hold me

hold me

LYRIC ESSAYS

jade vine

SPLIT LIP PRESS

Published by Split/Lip Press
PO Box 27656
Ralston, NE 68127
www.splitlippress.com

ISBN: 978-1-952897-39-9

Cover Art: Alexandra Eldridge, www.alexandraeldridge.com
Cover and Book Design: David Wojciechowski
Editing: Lauren Westerfield

*If you ever woke up
in the middle of the night
and prayed to a god
you didn't believe in,
this is for you.*

Every morning I walk like this around
the pond, thinking: if the doors of my heart
ever close, I am as good as dead.
Every morning, so far, I'm alive.

      —**Mary Oliver**, *from* Landscape

I was blinded like that—and swam
In what shone at me

only able to endure it by being no one and so
specifically myself I thought I'd die
from being loved like that.

      —**Marie Howe**, *Annunciation*

I wrote this poem to avenge myself against
desire, which made a fool of me.

      —**Aria Aber**

TABLE OF CONTENTS

SWANSONG

Sahiba and I are both in love. In the afternoon, we watch the rotis rise on the tawa, hot, our necks sweat sweet. When she presses her ears against the coldness of the floor, she tells me she can hear the names of all the people who died before her. She picks all the blue flowers first, then she eats each one. Every bite, she marvels, her tongue names a laugh and a scream.

&

Off-white, I mutter under my breath. The wall standing against the brief history of my body has always been this colour. Under the bedroom lights, I could've been praying for what looked like paper, crumpled, or a hand wrapped against its own. Under the bedroom lights, I have always been five and my mother is having a panic attack. I watch her in silence, then confusion. Mostly, I watch her in tears. I don't know what I look like when I have a panic attack, but maybe I look like her, scared, drowning in breaths, the kitchen doorway wet with tears.

&

My eyes move where she moves and where she doesn't. We are in the garden, we are standing in a line: an order of shrubs. I swear they couldn't tell us apart. I was barely eleven. How can you look death in the eye and be certain it hasn't come for you?

&

The first people to leave in history never left. They died right there, at that spot. Everybody else must've thought they were sleeping. Their loved ones watched them decay, bloodbones turned to dust. They didn't know it was death but they still cried. My dadi died in 2017, hundreds of years away from the first death in history. That night I cried. I cried because my father cried. I don't remember if I loved my grandmother then but now when people ask, I say *I do*.

&

I could've been sleeping when I heard my mother's voice coloured blue in rage. I don't resent her because I know her. The sorrow inheritance passed down through generations. In the afternoon, I watch her in the kitchen. The roti lands perfectly on the tawa and that's the only consolation in years spent loving everybody but ourselves.

&

The showerhead has been broken for the longest time. Mother tells me to leave broken things alone. She thinks if we can't bring them back, eventually we'll learn to live without them. Most of my nightmares end with me choosing to jump off a burning building. I could look for hidden meanings in my dreams, signs of despair, symptoms of ruins. But like many others, I choose to forget.

&

Mom, I'm sad and I don't think you can help.

&

I shave my legs, look out for signs of broken glass, tempered glass, glass paintings in churches. My hands shake the first day of summer goodbye.

In the backseat of the car, riding to Delhi, I clench my fists exactly forty-five times, letting go on forty-six.

&

Nobody will truly accept you but me.

Ma, was it easier for you to love me when you had me convinced no one could love me better?

At age sixteen, I'm in love with a boy I meet online. The boy tells me he loves me best. The boy tells me we're meant to be. Not even the gods are immune to confessions. Like them, even when my world is burning, I would've accepted a matchbox too.

&

Sahiba asks me three important questions. And none of the questions, she tells me, can be answered. These are the first few spells. We are on the kitchen floor, biting each other's nails. We both say *Mirza* and our voices crackle with intense pleasure. When we say *desire*, what we mean is *surrender*.

&

Inside my room, I flip through *Crush*: "If you love me, Henry, you don't love me in a way I understand." Time and space move, not just you and me. Are we, at any point in time, allowed to give up on understanding people? I don't want to know. Instead, mother, I hope *one day, love will not be too much, for either of us.*

&

Sahiba and Mirza died years ago. One minute, they are breathing, and then the next, there is nothing left to hide behind. No history is merciful. When Sahiba was not there, I imagined her in our bedroom. The next morning, I crawl on all fours. My mother calls me a liability and I am so close to screaming at her self-portraits but I don't. The silence stays between us like unimaginative crops, thick and blooming. Wherever we go, the light outside the room consumes us whole. The light outside consumes us before we can name it in a prayer.

&

The first order of the universe: good daughters don't tell their mothers what to do. I listened until my ears pressed so hard against the ground all I could hear was myself. It's impossible to forget I'm the bad seed. My mother cries to me in bed, *I'm sorry I say mean things to you, I know you're depressed but I am too*. The more we apologize, the further we find ourselves from it until we are so far, momentarily, everything disappears. My mother was no longer my mother. I, no longer her daughter. We became two mountains of adamant, so big we can't see the sun.

&

If I'm lucky, my mother will let go of her fears before I can outlive all of mine.

&

At night, once, I joked about dadi's spirit coming to see us. But when I heard footsteps, I curled into the bed, my mother's feet warming mine in the thick of winter.

&

If I think my mother is tired of looking at my face, sad and gloomy, a sore-riddled wake, then she is. By afternoon, I tell her *I want to die before she does*. She says she'll die before me anyway so it doesn't matter what I want. I never speak of Sahiba anymore.

&

Every day my mother tells me she'll be fine even if I didn't love her, as long as I don't hate her. Could god be something like her? Something achingly brilliant, but so scared?

&

I'm six. I wake up to the sound of my parents fighting—loud thunderclaps under the staircase. Once, the doorbell caught fire. We drew lights, burnt incense sticks, and cursed cutlery. In the house, I grew up a fire-extinguisher. Fifteen years of experience in *fuck-this-shit* and *I'll-take-care-of-it*.

If I die today, my mother will be inconsolable. If I die seventy years from now, will she welcome me home?

&

At age eleven, I'm drawing eyes on every notebook, father's diary, kitchen recipes, old wooden boxes, white walls. Nothing is outside my reach, even suffering, small and ugly in my hands.

&

My mother fears god, fears I'm going to run away, fears all my poems are sad poems, in that order. She is not wrong.

&

People would've accused Sahiba of killing her brothers too. People would've accused Sahiba no matter who died. Sahiba, I'm a scapegoat in this story and if I am to make it alive, home is not a place I want to be in.

&

At age fourteen, I make it a point to recite Warsan Shire poems to my mother. I read lines out of context to fit my own: *no one leaves home unless home is the mouth of a shark*. I'm convinced I'm shameless. The boy online already knows I don't have any friends.

&

Sahiba, lover of lovers, my awakening. My less-than-kingly arms fold at your touch. Love with me a hundred times more. I'm—

&

I'm a loser, my first crush was right. Except my first crush never called me a loser. My only consolation: I'm disgusted with myself. I write my name over as many things as you can imagine and then I cross it out.

&

I hang my feelings in alphabetical order: *anger, anger, anger*. The house begins to resemble my father's fists, my brother's fists, my mother's fist. We have so much in common. I hear it on the news next. Each day, for a year, I kiss the kneeling figure, the body in prayer, her feet littered with medical bills, food coupons, and the last ticket to the best show on earth. *Sahiba, you can come home now.*

&

People tell me I look a lot like my mother, her face my touchstone. Over the phone, people mistake us for the same person, almost. Two soft backs leaning against each other. When she holds my hands, I become her. Her arm swaying in the air, a faint outline of what I may become or who I already am.

&

Sahiba, ਮਾਸ਼ੂਕ ਧੋਖੇਬਾਜ, "beloved cheater." At age fifteen, I learn this is an oxymoron.

&

At sunrise, I offer my head, to be crowned or buried. *Sahiba, they cannot imagine me choosing both*. At age twenty, my mother and I cannot stop fighting and my father is still my father.

&

The summer is too hot and I'm without a friend. In the evening, I list all the irrelevant things to make myself seem more interesting. I'm not very tall. I like mangoes. I stole lemons from someone's garden when I was a child. This is my becoming, a ghost boy in love. Like the swans, I'm ravenous.

&

My mother and I sit next to each other, angry in our hand-me-downs. Our grey hairs and old regrets resurface. None of us pretend we can't hear it when we do so clearly. God's sermon, mustard seeds crackling in the pot, our voices burning like incense sticks. We retreat into our bedrooms, our lights still blue. Except I stand outside every door that opens, and she never leaves.

Notes

Sahiba is one of the titular characters of the story Mirza Sahiba, one of the five popular tragic romances in Punjab, who is wrongly accused of betraying her lover, Mirza.

8

I GET IT BUT YOU MUST NOT MISTAKE BLOOD FOR WARMTH AND LIGHT FOR LIFE

I GET IT YOUR FACE IS YOUR FACE IS YOUR MOTHER'S FACE IS ALSO YOUR FATHER'S FACE BUT I'D RECOMMEND YOU TO GO OUTSIDE

PLEASE GO OUTSIDE AND LOOK AT THE MOON AND ALLOW THE MOON TO LOOK BACK AT YOU

HOROSCOPE FOR MONDAY

Dear Sagittarius,

You did not drink from the bottle of water for the fear you might have none left. You thirsted like a little child, you made a sound for the language you did not speak, "mum-mum." The scientist Friedrich August Kekulé claimed to have discovered the ring structure of benzene after dreaming of a snake swallowing its own tail: the ouroboros. It was in a dream that your father died and resurrected. It was in a dream that the person you loved left you. It was in a dream that Dmitri Mendeleev saw the complete arrangement of the elements in the periodic table. You wake up with a mouth for hunger and you do not kill. You shoved the good girl in the memory and watched her die. No, you're still not scared of your dreams. Yes, that is your blessing and your curse.

THE MOON IS BEAUTIFUL, ISN'T IT?

In Ludhruva, the night was beginning to feel heavy. Imagine a stone in a raised fist. The birds belted out a long sigh before disappearing into the crater in the mattress, now visible with the body as evidence. Imagine when Momal looked up to the moon and could no longer bear the weight of her hands in submission.

&

A decade and a half ago, S is walking under the moonlight sky in the streets of Santa Fe in New Mexico. I have not been to Santa Fe, let alone any American city. In my bedroom, around midnight, I google: "nights in Santa Fe." This is the closest we've been in the past twenty-four hours after matching on Hinge. I'm time-traveling into the past while he waits in the present. Google has convinced me: Santa Fe looks just like he had described. *Best full moon nights*, he added. Tonight, I'll take his word.

&

Tonight, I have pulled his memory into my hands and opened the door to the balcony to peek at the moon, in Chandigarh, from about fourteen years back. I look at the moon, this breast of devotion, and say hello in the voice I inherited from my mother. My mother said hello and yes to my father in the same breath when they met for the second time, two years before I was born.

&

Hello is one of my favourite words in the language. One May night, lying next to the boy I have a crush on, I tell him: *People say hello to almost mean "I'm here," "I'm here in this room," "I'm here on this line waiting to talk to you," "Are you there?" "I miss you, wish you were here, " or "I want to hear you."* I tell him how every hello I've ever said was laced with want. In the morning, he turns his face towards me and says hello. I smile and say hello. What I'm really saying is: *I'm so close, so close. Can you feel breath, too?*

&

It is a dangerous territory. I forget all my gods, even the important ones. I'm looking at him with my mother's eyes, every tear of suspicion falls down my cheek like a silk ribbon, purple in all the right places. When I turn towards him, I have my father's plain face, no glimmer. Every touch then makes me more beautiful than I am. I have been told I look miraculous in grief. One of my older lovers said to me: *Yes, your mother was right. You do look beautiful when you cry. But please don't?*

&

Please don't leave. I'm not terrified of being alone, but I'm terrified nonetheless. I'm terrified of the moving insect, its tiny body tracing every inch of the floor I slept on, in your bedroom. The humming sound from the belly of the animal I'm scared to meet eyes with. I'm terrified of the man who calls me beautiful just the same. God knows what I'd do. God knows I've pulled my legs around my own head to know what it feels like to hold and be held in the same language. God knows nothing about this language, its ordinary, mutilated feelings. These days I am filled with them. All of my feelings are compressed into a memory of me falling from a height. The distance is always the same. I am on the ground and I am falling back into the sky.

&

"I almost wish / I'd never seen the sky / when always there was you. Sincerely," (Keith S. Wilson).

&

Tonight, he doesn't know how easy it is to fall in love. Or maybe he does. Is it giving him too much credit if I say he knew what he was doing? The thing is: I do not care. It was morning, the sun was out, I was breathing my body down into an eclipse: closing off back and forth, then suddenly. I do not care. It was the first morning of a small admission, a confession that I'm holding between my hands, tightly but not unwilling to let go. I'm threatened by the morning. But I do not care. All I know is that when he parted his lips, there was an ordinary sigh, a familiar word. The first word in the language: *Hello*. I do not care much for the morning. All I know is that of all the things in the room then, his face was turned towards me.

&

One of my closest friends tells me I have a habit of making things seem grander than they are. Is it a folly? Is it a gift? The zodiac tells me this is peak Sagittarius behaviour. My memory tells me another thing: I am waiting to be convinced that I'm beautiful, too. But let me be clear. The thing is: I have no shame in being ugly. Please let me make those grating sounds you hate, let me be the reason you turn your face away. Please let me be ugly. The thing still is: I wonder what someone who believes they're beautiful when they're told so feels about everything. I think about all the things and the people I've heard called beautiful.

&

In middle school, I'm sitting opposite a boy. I must tell you: I liked him very much then. I'm telling him about this girl who had just moved into the neighbourhood. I'm telling him how beautiful she is. I must tell you: I had a crush on her, too. I looked him in the eyes and described her the way one describes possibilities, in their immense bludgeoning—utter chaos and terrible beauty. He is listening to me, patiently and in earnest. It is so quiet, I can hear him listen. *She is beautiful.* I insist one more time, and he colours my neck pink with his first and only question: *Even more than you.*

&

Everything seems elaborate in someone else's hands. He places his hand against the wall, surely to support it. She keeps one hand on the table to steady it, another under her left cheek sitting across from me. I am the kneeling figure, my hands pressed against the floor, in submission. I'm the drool on the poster of a painting originally housed in a warehouse, now in a museum I'll probably never visit. On the ride back to North Campus, at night, in the auto, I stretch my hand between us. He lifts his hands from his lap like a child pulling the earth from under her for the first time, both in awe and unfazed, as if the miracle was a matter of fact but a miracle nonetheless. Until then, I did not think he could see me. Until then, I did not know he was looking.

&

In the morning, when Rano arrives, he finds another in Momal's bed. He mistakes them for her lover and leaves for Umerkot. He does not yet know it is Somal. Momal could not sleep without Rano so she had her sister pretend to be him. Is it not desire's most wretched form, to be so consumed by its own body that you are willing to risk the accusation of betrayal?

&

I have prayed. Please make me light or its burden. Let me burn, if I must. Please make me the spectator or a spectacle. Look with me or at me, I do not care as long as you look. Please find me a place where I can rest these hands or where I can rest. I do not care: I simply want to wish one goodnight as they offer me sweet dreams. God knows I have prayed. Please make these hands useful. Touch me. Allow me to touch you.

&

One too many times, I have waved at strangers, my hands moving midair like a church-bell stunned by its own bright burning. I have borrowed these hands, so much unlike my own, from a moment in time when my body was much closer to the sea than I had let on to the audience. The sea is the most dangerous animal. It is named after looking, an act, a preservation. It is its own witness. Tell me if that doesn't scare you.

&

The first night of July 2018, I'm alone and scared. But I'd choose fear over going back to my parents. I'd choose a thousand terrible nights that I can't sleep in Delhi over the one where I wake up in Chandigarh to find my body stationed at the foot of a moonless god's throne. I'm not saying I hate the city. But I'm not saying I love it either. I'm not saying Rano hated Umerkot. I only insist that there's someone waiting for us. I look up in the sky to find the face of the moon turned towards me, as if inching in for a kiss on the cheek. I want to lean in, against gravity, and choose catastrophe. I want one unending kiss under the moonlight. But all I receive is the night, its dark, merciless body shoved into my hands.

&

Imagine this: The balcony turns into an explosion of white. You're watching the first star in the sky fall towards the earth, its face vanishing before you can even kiss it. You assume nobody but you has seen the rot, this hunger pedal into the soft ground. You are certain it has placed its feet first into mud, then a field of jasmine, all plain-faced like your father before you. You are sure this means one thing: Every touch is devastating. Even a brush against the shoulder in the corridor, the gentle pat on your arm. Even this sleight of hand. Your feathers are all ruffled now. You're back in your room, under the blanket, looking at your hands with a torchlight and whispering to them: *Hello*.

&

When I was about six, the girls in my class showed me how to pull the half-moon down and into our palms. The girls insisted, then, that this half-moon hints at marriage with a beautiful person. I do not think about marrying. But I do bring my hands together and picture the face of the sky: the crescent moon. Then I remember all the beautiful people I have met. I remember their faces bright and burning, so bright that sometimes I have to turn away to really look.

&

When Momal wakes up to find Rano's cane, she fears he is never returning. Suddenly she is too bright for him to want to look her way. "If equal affection cannot be, / Let the more loving one be me" (W.H. Auden). In this moment, I know she loves him more. It is enough to meet your glance, it is enough, I console my heart. Let the more loving one be me, I console my heart. I console my heart because I cannot search Umerkot for Rano, I can only wait for him. I do love waiting, I tell the boy who apologizes to me for taking longer than he had expected. I'm no longer Rodin's Eve.

&

Rodin's Eve is a physical manifesto of remorse. A quick Google search will tell you she is despairing after the Fall. Yes, she is despairing, I will agree, but it is not the Fall, I will add. Eve holds her body in anguish and her face captive. I am sure it could only point to one thing. Every time I have looked at her, I have seen myself in a mirror, crying over unreturned love, lost love, never-mine love, it-could-be-mine-too love. Momal's face drew the moon's white when she woke up and realized Rano came and left. I saw that face, too. I could recognize Eve's lamenting posture anywhere in the world. This figure of yearning. What else could it be? What else but pure, ugly want? Her face screams nothing but this: *Tell me. Tell me you want it, too.*

&

I want love, I shout at the top of my lungs one night when I'm out with my friends, drinking. All my friends are drunk and I am the sober one. They are shouting to the moon. The moon, I'm afraid, isn't a good listener. But these people I'm riding the auto with are. One of them throws the question into the small space marked by a yielding to loss: *Why are they obsessed with love?* Hush, you do not say. Yes, I'm fairly familiar with my feelings. Yes, I am tempted by them too. Yes, I am the Heathcliff in this story calling out to all my dead and undead lovers in a prayer to a sober god. "They say I killed you, haunt me then. Be with me always. Take any form, drive me mad, but do not leave me. Not in a place where I cannot find you. I cannot live without my life. I cannot live without my soul," writes Emily Brontë in *Wuthering Heights*. Is this what Qais felt driven to madness in love? Is this what I want? To the onlooker, I bring my lips together to speak. To the spectator, I bring my lips together to kiss. Surely, touch is a language, too, felt all the same.

&

Natsume Soseki supposedly translated the English "I love you" into Japanese: 月が綺麗ですね, "Tsuki ga kirei desu ne." This translates to "the moon is beautiful, isn't it?"

&

In the winter of 2021, I meet someone online. *Look*, I say. *The moon is beautiful, isn't it?* They nod. We share pictures of the moon on WhatsApp.

At night, sometimes, they ask me: *Have you seen the moon tonight?* When I say I haven't, they send me a picture of the moon from their terrace. I take this gift and I am allowed to believe that that's the prettiest moon I have seen.

&

I know dadi pulled the moon out of dadu's name. She called him "Chan," which is the Punjabi word for moon. After dadi died, Gurbachan has not seen the moon the same way. After dadi died, the sky has been moonless.

&

A lover used to call me *moonpie*. Then he hurt me. I will not say anymore.

&

There was a crescent waning moon in the sky the night I was born. Many would tell you: the light was dimming, the sky was tempted. How it closed itself, mid-flight, around its own fingers to hold on to the less-than-bright things. We can't look at bright things without turning away. Many would tell you: it was dark. Many would tell you: the sky was unremarkable.

&

My mother tells me: *The moon was beautiful that night.* And I reply: *Wasn't it?*

&

Of all the Gods, Anteros scares me the most. He is the god of requited love, or love returned. Some say he was given to Eros as a playmate because Eros was lonely. Others say he arose out of the mutual love between Poseidon and Nerites. If the former is true, I think I can begin to understand when he first chose to punish those who scorn the advances of others. I do want my love returned, but I do not wish to be punished for not returning it. Plato notes in *Phaedrus*: "When he is with the lover, both cease from their pain, but when he is away then he longs as he is longed for, and has love's image, Anteros (love against love) lodging in his breast, which he calls and believes to be not love but friendship only, and his desire is as the desire of the other, but weaker; he wants to see him, touch him, kiss him, embrace him, and probably not long afterwards his desire is accomplished." Probably not long afterwards his desire is accomplished. Probably not.

&

I have been waiting in the wrong room all along. I need to be in the right room. Or at least outside the door of the room you stand in. Roland Barthes, in *A Lover's Discourse*, writes: "Every passion, ultimately, has its spectator…(there is) no amorous oblation without a final theatre." I stand under the setting sun, looking for Anteros's arrow overhead, and remember Shiv Kumar Batalvi's poem: ਆਜ ਦਿਨ ਚੜ੍ਹਿਆ ਤੇਰੇ ਰੰਗ ਵਰਗਾ, / ਤੇਰੇ ਚੁੰਮਣ ਪਿਛਲੀ ਸੰਗ ਵਰਗਾ, / ਹੈ ਕਿਰਨਾ ਦੇ ਵਿਚ ਨਾਸ਼ ਜੀਹਾ, / ਕਸਿ ਚੱਬਿ ਸਾਪ ਦੇ ਡੰਗ ਵਰਗਾ, "The day rose in your colour, / In the colour of your blush when I kiss you, / Even the rays dance appear intoxicated, / As if bitten by a venomous snake." I do not care. It is morning and the sun is out and everything in this world has its face turned towards me. I do not care for anything else. I know this, too, could be love. I know I will not have to die.

&

Tonight, I'm walking with my friends in Mandi House towards Bengali market. I'm holding hands with a friend as I cross the street. Another friend the next day sends the picture: it's me and him, walking on a road that doesn't know what hit it. Is it a body? A scavenge? Is it the swarm of ghosts? Does the road know where it's leading us or itself? I insist: *Please take me somewhere. Lead me on if you must. But take me somewhere.* The next two mornings, I'm still looking at this picture of us. The streetlight parts the branches of the tree to reveal its face. If I didn't know any better, I would've called it the moon, too. If I didn't know any better, I would have been certain it was the only moon in the universe.

Notes

Momal Rano is a love story from Sindhi folklore. It forms a part of the seven popular tragic romances from Sindh, Pakistan.

YOUR BODY IS A BODY IS A BODY IS A BODY

*WITH A GUN AND NO HEAD WHERE ARE YOU
AIMING*

*CUPID'S HEAD IS SO SMALL BUT YOU NEVER
MISS*

HOROSCOPE FOR TUESDAY

Dear Sagittarius,

Your body is not the only proof. Look what desire does to you even before it is done trying. You thought the small fence in my dream meant something safe and honest. But maybe the fence represents nothing but the fence. Today you dream cursive like your Punjabi. Your hands hold what you thought you could not: a boy in the summer of July, a girl in school you imagined killed you in a dream, a dream about your father you do not claim, your mother standing in the kitchen with nothing to hold on to but her loneliness. If you believe the Heisenberg Uncertainty Principle that observing something changes it, then it's no longer you in the photograph of him you keep. You know god is not the only witness.

MISDIAGNOSIS

OVERVIEW

You would've run it into a wall if you cared too little or too much. You don't know what is enough and neither does anybody else. You woke up one night crying, praying to a god you didn't believe in. Please. *Please. Please make it stop.* You were angry at god and he was just there. He was there but wasn't listening after all. Your body, with all its razor-sharp ways, was only a poor companion, it could not sleep without placing its hand on your mouth. Your mouth was a cave, an opening. It was never an exit. You've hungered your hands into desperation. Your hands have struggled to hold your heart in place, too heavy for all this blood. Sometimes, you choke on your spit.

SYMPTOMS

- Sensory overload: You are at the hospital, watching them take your mother into the ER. You know you will see her again but you do not know when. You know you have your whole life ahead of you—its newer gifts, strange men, petty propositions lined up at your doorstep. You think you want this life. This is a mistake. You think you don't want this life. This is a mistake, too. Everything is a mistake if it makes you feel any better. Everything is a mistake until it brings your mother back into your arms. Or brings you into hers. Before they pull her into the wheeled stretcher, your mother is still screaming. You watch her in awe. You watch her and you wonder if there is anything louder in this world, so loud you can hardly hear yourself over your own breath.

- Restlessness: You are fidgeting and irritable. It is quiet when he is sitting next to you and it is maddening before it is terrifying. He did not seem to understand or pick up on the hints. Or worse, he did. He did and he doesn't care and you're scared of wanting him anymore at all. You are disgusted with all this want that haunts you like the promise of a bruise or the bruise itself. You do not want to look at yourself in the mirror, afraid you're becoming so much more like the man who chased after you. Afraid the light that drove you into darkness has now forever marked your body as a gracious host. Afraid you are indeed the big bad wolf, you do not smile anymore. Afraid they might see the animal that you've been keeping at bay all your life.

- Itching: It grows hungrier inside your hands. First, it becomes the shadow of the lamb, then the lamb itself. This lamb you brought home. It hopped from one foot to another. You were sure he was your friend. You were sure he was harmless. You kissed him goodnight and clean. You licked the dirt off his cloven hoofs. It was nice imagining the little thing being good. You imagined the little thing was good in bed and you worried into a cold sweat. Now you worry your own language is the butcher's language. You worry that if you shear the lamb, you're taking your coat off. Of course, you're undressing. Of course, everybody has already seen you naked.

- Ear pain: You cannot hear. Or can only hear in murmurs, whispers, and pourings. You've poured too much into the cup and it's overflowing. This is the first sign to run, far and fast. You start with his head in your lap. You say to his face: *I miss you. I miss you so much.* It looks like he is listening intently. Then he turns his face away and you're no longer sure if he loves you. You're no longer sure you love him. Except you're crying and you're wishing your mother could be wrong about everything but especially about saying: *nobody will truly accept you but me.* Soon every man begins to look like your mother. You begin to look like your father. This is the second sign. You know why this is wrong. You make a prayer and tell everybody this is where you dwell now except you have never left the hiding. You make a prayer for him, inconsolable. Then you remember what the prayer is and your hands start bruising from its weight.

- Chafing: It begins with a walk in the garden. You've walked with men in daylight and at night. You've watched the curtains

announce the end of the scene and you've kept going. You've
watched yourself in disgust, taking to the corner. You've promised the person in the mirror you'd follow him anywhere he
went. You follow him out of the garden. Your thighs begin to
chafe and you do not complain. You'll do it for a few extra minutes with him. You're bleeding and you'll do it for an hour.

- Wrist pain: Your mother waited so long to be kissed. Then she
  moved her face—first towards the lantern, mistaking it for your
  father's. The first love letter she wrote she told you resembled
  the belly of a wolf. She told you if the envelope paper pressed
  against her lips tasted like anything, it tasted like surrender. She
  didn't tell you about her hands.

- Mouth pain: You haven't sucked his dick in a long time. You're
  having withdrawal symptoms. Even brushing your teeth makes
  you gag. You're afraid of swallowing pills so you stop taking your
  medication altogether. The men in your bed last night did not
  hesitate to call you crazy. It doesn't matter, you tell the damp and
  frothy fingers that run over your face. Your psychiatrist thinks
  you're insane even though she doesn't say it. It doesn't matter.
  You have tried convincing her this was love, too. Except you forgot to convince yourself. The faint outline of your body on the
  bed is drawn with chalk.

- Insomnia: I am afraid of everything I have seen. How could I
  sleep at night? How could I place the child into the wastebasket? I want to forget my father, I want to forget how he hurt my
  mother. But then I remember his face as lonely as a city and I
  wonder if maybe both of us are lost.

- Hypersomnia: You are convinced the ghosts of the people you
  love come into your bed and warm up against the small of your
  body. You do not want to walk away from this miracle that god
  forgot to announce to his rookie angels and now apparitions
  walk the earth and nobody mentions them.

- Hand tremors: You were a child holding the little bird, a golden
  chick, your hand sways in the distance imitating time with its
  endless pursuits. You were sure the bird was sleeping in your
  hands. Years later they tell you the bird died in your hands. You

had carried its soft body everywhere for hours. You carried it thinking there was life beating its small body. Your body is the first site of death before you pull your arms around him, ever-so-slightly, now pressed into your chest as you collapse. The little bird would've died within weeks but you couldn't have then known that it was your hands. Your hands: a crime scene. Your hands: the death bed. Today you are afraid to want something. Today you are afraid to touch your lover's face.

- Sadness: You are insufferable in so many ways. You have been so lonely. You have walked into the arms of men who you admit you knew would hurt you. You do not know whether to name this act preservation or self-destruction but you name it regardless, hoping if it has a name, it has a purpose and you can walk away from it, too.

DIAGNOSTIC CRITERIA

What comes first: desire or loneliness? You are the captor, holding your body hostage. Natalie Wynn, the creator of the YouTube Channel "ContraPoints," explains masochistic epistemology: *whatever hurts is true*. Your father calls you a whore, your mother calls you a liability. Your lover once called you *dirty* in the same language. Doctors advise against licking your own wounds like a dog, but we all do. You tongue yourself in the room while everybody watches from a distance. There's enough distance, you'll kill yourself over it.

PREVALENCE

When stars exhaust and die, they burn everything into iron. The lab reports suggest your body has sufficient iron. You imagine, then, you're dying, too. There's a word for "the contemplation of dust," or what has been lost. *Dustsceawung*, they call it. You watch the world as the dust settles on your body in the thick of the wind.

COMORBIDITIES

You learned from your mother. She would cut fruit into tiny pieces and bring a piece to you to eat. You insist she loves you. Today, you use the knife like your mother, steady, you peel the skin off the mango, leaving only the seed. You hold the knife with so much care and disbelief. Your psychiatrist calls it self-harm. You call it making breakfast.

TREATMENT

If you are to be no longer ashamed and no longer alone, you must begin by imagining them imagining you. You must not begin with a stiff face and you must not look away. Your mother will call you on the phone. Do not pick it up. Do not suppose it is all the faces of the men who've hurt you when the morning begins with a face full of stitches. It is too quiet and too gloomy where you're at but that is not a promise. There is no promise of tomorrow. Only heads burrowed and bountiful. You will hold your head like a small handkerchief you're waiting to lend to some-one. You will finish your breakfast. You will disassemble your bed. You will whistle your favorite song and then you must forget all about it. You will kiss many men and women and sometimes it will taste disturbingly sweet. You will love many people and sometimes they will love you back.

STRATEGIES FOR LIVING WITH WHAT YOU IMAGINED HAD KILLED YOU MONTHS AGO OR WHAT YOU IMAGINED YOU COULD NOT LIVE WITHOUT

There will be love or another door that leads you back to the garden in your grandmother's house in the summer of 2006. You will open your hand and take the full bush of yearning. You will hold it without throw-ing up on your clothes. Love comes and you only have to receive it today.

YOU CAN BE CRUEL AND YOU WON'T LIKE IT AND

IT'S NOT WORTH IT AND YOU CAN BE CRUEL AND SOMETIMES

YOU WILL BE AND WHEN YOU'RE FINALLY CRUEL YOU

MIGHT

SEE THE WORLD FROM WHERE YOUR

FATHER STANDS AND TRUST ME WHERE YOUR FATHER STANDS IS NOT THE GROUND AND THE GROUND WHERE YOUR FATHER STANDS ON CAN NOT SHOULDER THE

WEIGHT OF CRUELTY AND YOU CAN BE CRUEL BUT

REALLY WHY WOULD YOU EVEN WANT TO YOU CANNOT TAKE

BACK THE WORDS YOU CANNOT CALL BACK THE RAINS

HOROSCOPE FOR WEDNESDAY

Dear Sagittarius,

You're afraid you have begun measuring the day by the number of hours you never see your mother. You have loved less & none so absolutely, in the throes of it, that sometimes there is a wrong answer. There is a wrong answer but mostly you hope you never know your moments of weakness again, the earth wound up against a small rock, fistful and none of that is science or helpful. You thought strangely, like your mother who has tried to be kind to you. You thought nobody would love you. Today you do not know how to be certain, not in the manner the oracles were, the harbingers of bad news, or the absolute worst of an equation. Your breath is patchy between syllables like it was decades ago, oscillating between unfashionable and vintage in your own skin. You're twenty-three and not a chin dipped in salted butter for you to lick here. It doesn't matter that all these years you have collected threads, their mangled confessions, and now you're coming undone at the whisper of your own name. Your hand is never static when you pick the poison, the ripened fruit, and you know all your gifts.

YOU'RE DANGEROUSLY LOW
ON SPACE

1. I cannot close my eyes and remember what I look like. It's been two weeks since I looked into a mirror. There's a mirror outside my room, bent and hollowed to keep me small. It's a good trick. I imagine I do not want to look at the wounds across my face. Barefaced into catastrophe. I was afraid I wouldn't recognise myself. Sometimes, I hear my voice over the phone and think it's a stranger. I hear my voice over the phone and I'm certain it's my mother's.

2. My mother discouraged us from keeping the door to the dressing room open when we went to sleep. The dressing room held the biggest mirror in the house. The mirror was bigger than my father's shadow sprawled across the pavement. I asked my dadi. She told me the spirits on the other side would suck my soul in. It was frightening. As a child, I fed on clever things, familiar things, fallow fields, faces shining bright in front of the mirror. I was afraid of what the mirror would show me. It was only frightening because I would've believed anything. I even believed my father liked me at all, once.

3. I should've been afraid of who I was. Should've looked twice at the person in the mirror before offering them a hand. I didn't know then that I was waiting to be sucked in. Translation: *Please look at me and stay there looking.*

4. I know very little about Theagenes. Except the story that Pausanias recounts. How Glausias of Aegina built a statue of Theagenes. And when Theagenes died, a man would go and beat the statue. One day, the statue fell upon the man and killed him. The Greeks put the statue on trial for murder and convicted it. They threw it into the sea. When the plague hit the city, the people went to consult the

Oracle at Delphi. Perhaps it is true. Perhaps they pissed off Theagenes. Perhaps that is why they went to pull the statue out of the sea. Perhaps they finally looked at themselves in the water this time when they did it, their faces little, so little.

5. Isn't pulling the same as pushing? When I went to drown in the bathtub, I was pulling myself out. When I kissed him, I was pulling myself in. When I ran in front of a moving car, I was pulling myself away. When I pushed the door, you were pulling it towards yourself. I never screamed or let out a sigh. I am the choir of animals singing the singular word. When he pulls my hands, I'm pushing them towards him. When I pull the moon into my hands, I'm pushing it back into the sky. In my darkest moments, I can still hear myself, the body opening like a fist at the end of the night spent against the body of night.

6. I was waiting at the bus stop, at night when it was raining, next to a man. I hardly knew him. I wonder if that's what a marriage is sometimes: sleeping next to someone you hardly know come morning. You might know them really well in the moment before you both become what the world needs. Then you turn towards each other. Then you know you're pulling away. My mother never described marriage like that. But she didn't have to. She didn't have to describe the rain for me to know it was pouring that night. That night, under the moonlight, the road was the glass slipper I pushed my body into. God knows I'm clumsy when I'm grateful just to come close to death.

7. My father, I want to argue, is no longer my father. But that doesn't change the translation much: the room was small, or my father was big. Time cradles in my arms but never touches me. I'm touched but not for love. I want to imagine my father mistook my mother. I want to imagine my father never hitting her. I want to imagine the room big or else I could've missed it. I gesture to the signs that point toward something important but I cannot remember what's important about them anymore. Whatever travels in straight lines, it was light, yes, but not always. I had imagined my mother leaving in the dark so many times before. She wakes up in the dull slivers, puts on her coat, picks up her bag, and calls the cab. It broke my heart and hers when it never happened. I watched my mother make the bed every day, mimic intimacy and risk exposure to light. I didn't fear running

away. All my life I only thought it was unfair. We should run away, but why should we? This is our home, too.

8. My mother doesn't call omission kindness but I know it. She tells me my father is a lovely man. She insists not on the *lovely* but the *father*. She tells me he is a lovely man and maybe clumsy. I used to think she meant how he had hit the mirror and missed. But now I think she meant he's missed a lot.

9. Words flash on my phone screen: *You're dangerously low on space.* I delete two apps to make space for one. The dating apps go. I'm trying to come home with these hands, I hit the power button and look at my father in the dark box or what has now become the phone screen. I look so much like him, I cannot help it. I look like him and I worry how I've never written him a poem. And I have written many poems before. I worry how none of the poems I've ever written are for him. I worry how they're all still about him.

10. I do not hate my father. If I do, then I must also hate myself. I am only as lovely as he is, if not more.

11. My father and I fight a lot behind closed curtains. One time, in a fight, I said something to him that I regretted almost immediately. I did not regret it because I didn't mean it. I regretted it because I meant it. Hardly a minute had passed. I hardly finished. I found the cruel bone: *I wished you were dead.*

12. When Dylan Corliss and Lexie Vaga were walking down Claremont, holding hands, lightning struck them. They could've died right at the spot. Dr. Stefan Reynoso explained that holding hands may have saved them. It dissipated some of the electrical voltage. I'll take his word. I would've still believed holding hands saved them even if no one said it. These days, when I'm in my room and he's not there to hold my hands, I feel like I've been struck by lightning. This is the future I'm running away from. I want to take my wounds and leave them for drying as I warm my body against his.

13. These days, when I'm traveling back alone towards Samaypur Badli, the last station on the yellow line, I am overcome with a familiar feeling. It is bright and blue and ugly and it makes me want to rip my insides out. I could've invented yearning if Sappho hadn't already.

But mostly I was scared of all the bodies inside me when I came up for air like a bag of helium balloons.

14. I was scared of balloons as a child. The balloon in the room, more green than possession, more ugly than spring's divine bosom, I never knew its next move. It was bigger than I was then. I was scared but not because the balloon was massive. I was scared because I know massive things. All of them named after the animal my father makes of me.

15. I'm the deer in headlights looking at the blood I have drawn with a kitchen knife like it was a promised word from the dictionary my mother lent me. I couldn't have coughed so much even if I tried. I didn't think I was so much blood at all. All bone but no mercy. I imagined my parents never threatening to call the cops on me. I imagined my father apologizing to me. I imagined him dressing my wounds. I imagined my mother curling up to me in bed. I imagined that I would no longer need to rely on my imagination to comfort me. I could not imagine anymore so I repeated: *I wished you were dead*. I repeated: *I'm never coming back*. I repeated to my lover: *I will never be my parents*.

16. A lover is looking at my face and I'm looking at the streetlights. I'm looking at the streetlights because I want him to look at me without having to worry that I'm looking at him too. I am not looking away. I am looking towards him, humbled by my own desire. I am looking at the moon at the back of my head and he's looking at me, and I'm hoping he can still see the moon. I know love has a right to be received.

17. In the last episode of *Fleabag*'s season 2, Fleabag looks at the Priest and offers him these words: "You know the worst thing is that I fucking love you." He responds with: "It'll pass". On the day of the father's wedding, the Priest says: "Being a romantic takes a hell of a lot of hope. I think what they mean is when you find somebody that you love, it feels like hope." It'll pass. It'll pass. I repeat to my parents. They stand with their backs turned towards the mirror.

*THE ONLY THING I HAVE FROM MY
GRANDMOTHER IS A BEAUTIFUL WATCH AND
THEN I GAVE IT AWAY TO A BEAUTIFUL BOY
WHO BROKE UP WITH ME ON A BEAUTIFUL
AFTERNOON AND THEN I THOUGHT I MISSED
MY GRANDMOTHER HER BEAUTIFUL FACE
BUT I THINK THEN I JUST WANTED THE
WATCH BACK I THINK THEN I HATED MY
FATHER MORE THAN I LOVED HER*

GRIEFDOM

I'm pulling my body like a thread through a needle. I'm trying to make something beautiful of my hands. I do not know how to spend my grief anymore. I'm saving it all up. To spend in my afterlife, at the end of life, or whatever I can still afford without giving up my hands or giving too much of myself away. I do not want to leave any room for interpretation: I want my grief to be as obvious as the knife blade kneading through the fish belly. But I don't look sad. Or sad enough.

&

And let's say, just maybe. Just maybe, I'm not sad. I feel like I'm already betraying her memory as the thought wheels through my mind. But she can't even remember, she is already gone. *Were the oranges sweet?* I wanted to ask her once. Maybe I can stop myself from longing without hungering my hands into roadkill. Maybe not. Don't 'maybe not' and 'maybe' mean the same thing? One evening, I watched dadi fold her many faces into a basket she brings over for lunch. She pulls out her favourite face and gives it to me. For a whole day, I'm her. Old, frayed, slumped between syllables, and for the large part, dead.

&

I was toying with her memory. Pulling it apart or bringing it together, it's hard to make out from a distance. C.S. Lewis, in his book *A Grief Observed*, discusses how he reinvents his dead wife in his mind. He knows the version of her that now lives with him is not her, not "in a word, real." I look at her picture in the photo album and wonder: how can someone be ugly and beautiful at the same time.

&

I do not recognize half the faces at the funeral. Green dupattas. Green salwar-kameez. Dadi wore a green suit in the photograph hung on the wall. They couldn't have known.

&

They couldn't have known how easy it was to recognize her in a crowd. I once watched her through the kitchen window, walking in the garden, her cane steadying her body like a prayer. It was the only time I remember she was suffering. It was the only time I remembered god.

&

I'm constantly thinking of a time forward in the future where she's still alive. Richard McNally and Don Robinaugh found in a study that people suffering from complicated grief had difficulty imagining their future without the deceased. Instead, they were able to imagine an alternate future that included their lost loved one. Because I yearn for that counterfactual future, a future where her hand still finds my cheek as my hand finds her at all. In my room, nine years from today, dadi places her hand on my shoulders as she counts the beads on the rosary. She asks me to accompany her to the gurdwara on a Sunday. I eat the churi she makes me for lunch. I trust her enough to hold her hands or whatever's left of them.

&

Dadi believed in god. Like he was real. Or made-up after something that was. When her breathing slowed, she is still chanting ਵਾਹਿਗੁਰੁ, "Wa-heguru." I wasn't there when she died. But I was there the one morning where she woke me up early, and she placed her hand on my chest. Her hand kept on pulling on my hair, gently. All this pulling to make sense of

44

what we cannot read in light. How can I even begin to tell her that I'm trying to love her less tonight.

&

The night dadi died, I—I cried, I cried because my father cried. I don't remember if I loved my grandmother then but now when people ask, I say *I do*. I was still pulling her in my memory, carrying her graceless rot, her thinning hair. Tahlequah, a twenty-year-old orca, carried the body of her dead 400-pound calf for seventeen days and 1,000 miles. The southern resident killer whale was grieving for its dead baby. She was not ready to let go.

&

I'm not ready to become a servant to my sadness. I have given this sadness many names. Last night it was so far up the road, it hadn't happened. Today it's my own hand fetching me from the kitchen, terrified of the body that hasn't collapsed yet. What I know is this: one afternoon, at a bookstore, I missed her. It was terrible. I puked after.

&

Phantom Limb syndrome: "a condition in which patients experience sensations, whether painful or otherwise, in a limb that does not exist." She is not here but her dupatta still stains my hands pink, fistfuls of what has passed in the flooded rice paddy or what I thought my father wouldn't notice. My grief, after all, isn't just my own. After all. And if not for my father, I wouldn't know dadi at all, her history laid before me like a mangled carcass. I wouldn't even know her name and I couldn't possibly imagine.

&

Gertrude Stein in "Portraits and Repetition" notes that "There's no such thing as repetition. Only insistence." Dadi believed my made-up stories, she looked at me enthusiastically, reaching for the first syllable of my name: tan. ਤਾਂ ਕਿ ਹੋਇਆ , "tan ki hoya," she insists. It's been four years and I've been asking myself the same question: *so what if it happened?*

&

I'm convinced she can catch my head into her lap. Except she isn't here anymore and I no longer think I can fit my whole body inside of her. This is a performance of grief, a scene in the final act.

&

Act I: elephants touch the corpse or old bones. They recognize the dead the same way they greet a newborn. Sometimes, the elephant returns to a place where a member has been buried.

Act II: when a pack member dies, the wolves walk slowly, their tails and heads hang low. It does not start with the "inner feelings of the bereaved" but, as Katherine Ashenburg notes, with "the mourner's dance."

Act III: Mostly, I look at the watch for years propped up on the wall. I look at the watch to find my father's face. I look at my father's face to find hers. Mostly, I have been trying to pull my hands outside my mouth. I want to find something else to call beautiful.

&

I want to confess. I cannot taste anything but the salt from her fingers I kissed. I want to confess. We do get to choose whom we love. This is why grief is terrible. I want to confess. Green is a terrible colour.

Notes
The line "How can I even begin to tell her that I'm trying to love her less tonight?" is a reference to Ada Limon's "dearest, can you / tell, I am trying / to love you less."

46

*THERE IS PAIN IN THIS WORLD BUT NOT WITH
YOU IN THE ROOM TONIGHT*

*TONIGHT I AM TRYING TO FOREGO MY BODY
AND I AM*

TRYING

*TO TELL YOU ALL ABOUT IT ITS CRACKS AND
VALLEYS AND*

CROOKED STREETS WITH BEAUTIFUL PEOPLE

*FORGIVE ME I'M HUMILIATED BY MY OWN
DESIRE TO BE HELD IN THE ARMS LIKE A
CHILD*

DEAR S. SO YOU MUST KNOW

There is a morning where your face swallows mine. We are two shadows, kissing the light pinned against the wall and I saw the knife you threw away. I saw the head and for a good reason, I am greedy, I tell the scientists. I want to gesture and sink low into the sky. You're trying to touch me how I want to be touched. I am at the door, you bend and hold my leg. I cannot worry my body into an empty room when I'm with you. You say to me, *don't leave. Come with me*, I say. *Come with me.* There is a morning where we repeat our bodies like overcoats. I come with my hands, outstretched and steady. You come with yours holding my face.

&

It's not a goodbye, you said. I do not think about it, not until I'm half-way across. I'm crying to a pop song. The passenger next to me is crying too, I imagine.

&

It is the beginning of July. Maybe it is the only summer in the decade. Songlike, incandescent, and terribly short-lived. I watched it, all shriveled inside my hands, cupped into a clarion call. M speaks to me about an old friend and a murder of crows. The old friend would sing to them and the murder would sing back to him. I called it beautiful before I learnt what it was. I know you would too.

&

On the flight back, I'm sitting behind a man who is scrolling through Instagram. He opens the profile of a beautiful girl. He is looking at her pictures. He opens each one, zooms in and out. He goes through her list of followers, carefully scouting for something that might make him feel less obsessive. Is this what I look like to the world? I did not want to think about him, especially because I could not help it.

&

I waited for you to arrive, like a season, I stood up with a terrible ache as I walked towards you, down the steps. Do people compare their lovers from the present with the past? I promise I'm not calling you a lover, unless. You walked with me over the tiny bridge, in your pink shirt, you held my left hand, then right. You knew I wanted a song. You knew I wanted to cover my face. In the city park, sitting in front of the pond, you lifted your shirt to show me the bruise on your back, all rose-coloured and blood. You told me you were drunk and you fell. You were laughing when you told me. I did not laugh. I flinched. I said *I'm sorry*. I stop only to look into your eyes.

&

You are walking me back, you say to me: *I just want to make you happy.* I want to distrust your words, frantically and hysterically, but you're so charming and your eyes glisten when you smile.

&

I could have sworn I invented the colour of the house you live in. I could have sworn it was my favourite, all washed up and hurtling between cyan and green.

&

When you turn your face towards the TV screen, I turn my face towards yours.

&

Are you evil? I say yes. I'm joking. *Do you want to be evil?* you ask me when we're walking to your house. I'm still holding your hand. *No*, I answer.

&

I was out of breath before I had even kissed you.

&

I did not admit to you: I was threatened to be seen before I could show myself. The first time I kissed you, I told you: *it's almost like you've never been kissed before*. Your lips are soft. So soft. I feared I might bruise if I kissed you. I kissed you still. I was an animal. And you were another.

&

There isn't a word in the language for the picture of the river I delete from my gallery, so I could keep yours.

&

For a brief moment, the light pouring from outside the window touches me the way a hand touches me, not just any hand, but someone I love, or if I'm lucky, my own. I'm sitting with three other people from the University of Iowa's Summer Institute cohort as we wait another hour before boarding. The first time I met you, it was incredibly warm, though not unusually warm for a summer day. I'm sinking into the light and I'm terrified I won't completely drown. I'm terrified someone will draw the blinds. At the airport, I tell M: *I'll come back*. M tells me: *I'll see you soon*. M is smiling. M might never know this: I will have never left even as I'm leaving.

&

You come see me at seven in the morning. We're sitting outside the Residence Halls. *It'll be a while*, I tell you when you ask when I'm coming back. I love the idea of returning. You return where you belong, don't you?

&

It is true that there are more trees on Earth than there are stars in the Milky Way. We are more likely to die in a car crash than a plane crash. I'm afraid you wouldn't like me if I had nothing to tell you anymore. I'm afraid the silence will kill me first before you hear it.

&

Fear, the verb, in Old Saxon, *faron*, literally means "to lie in wait." I fear. I lie in wait. The Proto-Indo-European root of fear, the noun, literally means "to try, risk." It is the fear. I have risked it all. When I met you, I had time. And now as I leave, I fear I have a whole life.

&

Here's a room troubling everyone a little less. Here's a room troubling me to my core. The only issue: you're not here anymore. All you wanted to say you didn't. All I wanted to hear I didn't. Maybe in some part of the timeline: what I want to hear and what you want to say overlap. I do not know the story and I am praying the maybe turns into a yes. I am praying the day we leave each other never returns. Let it be known: loneliness is not welcome in this room. Last night in bed I said *I'm lonely*. I meant *I miss you*. I want the dance to be your body. I want to take this room and all eyes on you. I want every door to open into your room. I want the door closed at night. Leave the windows open. Let the rain come in. Let the jasmine fill the air. Let me hear the trees moan as I do.

&

We are in June. My friend A tells me as I'm crying. A is drunk. But that is beside the fact. A isn't looking into my eyes. A doesn't need to but insists on it. A has seen my eyes. Not a deer in the headlights. Not a moment before its passing. A knows my eyes. A is certain the lemon is sour and the beer good. A repeats in the clearest words. A tells me I have the brownest eyes—the brownest eyes ever to brown. I do not remember my eyes when I'm looking into yours. Your eyes are brown—more brown than the brown looking back at me in the mirror.

&

Whatever sport you play I want to play. I want to kick the ball in your opposite direction. I want to throw the punch when you do not duck. I want to run, pin you to bed. I want them to replace the sound of rain pouring with the sound of your laughter. I want the world to know you and keep you like fire. Whether god wills it or not, I will see you next summer. The next summer will be golden. The next summer will not end how we want it to. The next summer will know it's come so far. The next summer glows with the knowledge that I wake up in the morning and find your face before I find mine.

&

If they look at me, they will know. They will know I'm the first symptom of ruins. I'm the first symptom of the body doing with desire what it knows. I'm the first symptom of language invented for the subject of one's affection. I'm the first symptom, yes. But not the only one. Not the only one, I hope

&

The story goes that after invading and taking control of Greece, Phillip II of Macedon sent a message to the Spartans: "If I invade Laconia, you will be destroyed, never to rise again." "If," the Spartans replied. *If.* S, if you wake up one day and you have nothing to say to me anymore. If we never meet again. I do not finish these sentences. But there is nothing to fear. That is the mercy of *if*: a gift we both give to each other.

&

I make you watch *Chungking Express*. I have already watched it. This is how the film ends: Faye, before leaving for California, leaves Cop 663 a boarding pass dated a year later. She returns to Hong Kong, now as a flight attendant. She meets Cop 663, at the snack bar she used to work at, who tells her he is turning the snack bar into a restaurant and the grand opening is in two days. She has an early flight and he asks her when she'll be back. "I don't know," she answers. "This might be a long trip." He pulls out the boarding pass she gave him, now all wrinkled. Faye offers to write him another one. She asks him where he wants to go. Cop 663 replies: "Doesn't matter. Wherever you want to take me."

When do you come back, you asked me a few days before. *It'll be a while*, I replied. The day I leave, I leave you with two bus tickets. One from Chandigarh to Delhi. Another from Delhi to Chandigarh. Do you know what it means, I wonder. Do you know I'll be back in a year?

&

In your room, we watch *Natural Born Killers*. The scene opens with Leonard Cohen's "Waiting For The Miracle." You have already watched the movie, years ago in fact. You want to watch it with me, this is not a miracle but I will take it. You want to watch the movie with me and I want to be beautiful in every room I am standing in with you. And aren't we the most beautiful when we're desperate? I am desperate to dissolve whatever distance there is between you and I. I'm welcome to ask questions, I know. But are you ready to be cruel? I'm sorry, I did not mean it that way.

&

I did not tell you everything. But I told you about my father.

&

I say *forgive me father*, I let the sea rise up to my waist. I let it dissolve between my thighs like thunder into the night sky. I say *forgive me father, I snuck the jasmines into the vase at night*. I let the house smell of a lover's ache. I say *forgive me father, I called the rain instead of calling your mother when she was still alive*. I say *forgive me father, if I could call upon from the grave, I would still call the rain*. I say *forgive me father, I am not ashamed of this desire. I am no longer ashamed to touch myself in my lover's image*. I say *forgive me father, I dig the holes poorly*. Even the dirt won't come out. I am here with a scalpel, making myself less like you. I say *forgive me father, I wanted you dead until the one evening I dreamt you were dying*. I say, *father, is this my evil?* I say *forgive me father, I loved you too*. I say *forgive me father, I might like a boy and he is not you*. I say *forgive me father for not forgiving you*. I say *forgive me father, I forgive myself.*

&

I dip the rusk in chai. I fold the laundry into neat piles. I mash the potatoes. I will even pick a fork. I will not close my eyes to tomatoes, crushed under the weight of time. I will watch the apple fall from the sky and bruise. You wouldn't believe the things I'd do to find the softest parts.

&

A series of selfish questions: If I had nothing to offer you anymore, would you still listen? If I disappear tomorrow, would you still carry me around? If you had to choose… I stop right there. I will never finish the question, I do not want to be cruel. It would be accurate to say too: I do not want you to remember me as cruel.

&

I will turn the lights on the next time.

&

"It's like you want to have the least sex-sex." I wasn't angry when you said that. You had nothing to apologise for and yet you did anyway; you still do. You couldn't have known about the men who hurt me, wound after wound. I sleep on the floor that night. In the morning, you ask me if you could join, I nod.

&

Do you remember me without my prompting? Do you still miss me even when I'm not texting *I miss you* first? It doesn't matter to the world what I'm about to do, but I'm waiting for you to call.

&

I bite your cheek and it leaves a soft, pink mark. The next day, we are back in your room. I am teaching you how to hold the knife, steady and patient, across my chest. I remember Casca's words to Guts: "I too want a wound that I can say you gave me." Your knives aren't sharp, we tell each other. But in the end, you simply do not want to hurt me because it hurts you too. I didn't say that but I wonder if I did.

You would add: *That's aggressive.*
You would chime: *That's cute.*
You would laugh into the mic: *You're wack.*

To an audience, the effect is underwhelming. But I'm not the audience. I'm on stage and the lights go out.

&

I miss you so much, my mouth swells with ache, I wish we'd never met.

&

On my last flight, I'm scrolling through Instagram. I'm looking at your pictures. I'm realising, finally, how utterly devastated I am. How desperate I am to close the distance between us. Now almost 7,456 miles. In your bed, you're holding me. But before I even know it, I am holding you back.

&

At my mother's house, I'm looking at the map of Santa Fe. I'm trying to memorise the names: Galisteo St, Chavez Pl, W Buena Vista St, Cam Adela, Anita Pl, Laughlin St, E Berger St, Pino Rd. I am tracing the hills of Sangre de Cristo with my fingertips, zooming in and out. I want to know the place you say you want to settle in.

&

Our texts are now far and few in between. Most of it is time.

&

तरसना, "to long, crave, or thirst." Tell me I'm not the only one suffering. Tell me tonight desire annihilates you too. Desire lines, Parker Schorr says, are "the living histories of travelers wandering off pavement, forming shortcuts, carving their own trails and recreating their communities." Tell me if every desire line isn't saying the same thing: *I want to walk there*. Tell me you see these lines. Tell me I'm not the only one.

&

The male anglerfish bites into the belly of the female anglerfish. He latches on until his body fuses with her. This practice confused scientists for the longest time, scientists who thought maybe this fused body was that of the female anglerfish's child or even a different species. Only later they discovered it was that of her mate. She invites him inside and he has chosen her to carry him. Now a single respiratory and digestive system. Now her eyes in the dark are all the light there is in the world. Now is this what it means to be made in your lover's image?

In 1938, William Beebe, a naturalist and marine biologist, wrote: "But to be driven by impelling odor headlong upon a mate so gigantic, in such immense and forbidding darkness, and willfully eat a hole in her soft side, to feel the gradually increasing transfusion of her blood through one's veins, to lose everything that marked one as other than a worm, to become a brainless, senseless thing that was a fish—this is sheer fiction, beyond all belief unless we have seen the proof of it."

How much more proof do we need, I ask, looking into the mirror.

&

You reply: *I long for you too*. You reply: *It's okay I just wanted to make sure you knew I knew*. If I didn't already like you, I would've liked you then

58

&

I prepare myself for the bullet: the unread texts, the left-on-seen texts
and the silence that accompanies it all, the loneliness of being the only
one who has feelings for the other. I keep asking my friends if I imagined it, meeting you and your hands on my face. I need a set of hands to
touch my face. Come over. It's nearing two weeks since I left the coun-
try. Tarot cards tell me to be patient, that I must preserve. That I must
praise the dirt that kisses my knees when I fall towards the pavement.
Forget all that. I'm asking you to be a burden to me, let me be the one
to carry. I want to be happy.

MY FRIENDS KNOW I FLINCH WHEN MY
FATHER RAISES HIS VOICE THEY KNOW MY
MOTHER MAKES FEEL SO LONELY

AND IF I LOVED MY MOTHER LIKE A FRIEND
AND IF I LOVED MY FATHER LIKE MY MOTHER
I WOULD TELL THEM ABOUT ALL THE
HEARTBREAKS AND ALL THE WAYS I

IMAGINED I WOULDN'T DIE AND DID

BUT I NEVER TELL THEM

FEAR IS A SMALL BOY HE WON'T LET MY
HAND GO

HOROSCOPE FOR THURSDAY

Dear Sagittarius,

You've been hearing the world is going to end, go up in flames. You heard it from your classmate in primary school. She said she heard it on the news, that tomorrow the earth will split open and let out fires. You never saw her after that. Maybe you simply cannot remember her beyond the end of the world. You decline the earth's sweet proposition: the end of the world. You have been crying and you'd think for someone who cries so much, they'd feel like a person at least but you haven't felt like one in a long time. The closest you came to feeling human was feeling humiliated by your own desires. You were so ashamed at wanting to be held. You should at least close your eyes when you kiss.

I MUST ASK YOU TO LOVE
IRRATIONALLY

a series of texts that were never sent

The first motion sensor was invented by Samuel Bagno in 1950. It used ultrasonic waves and the Doppler effect to detect motion. But since the ultrasonic waves could be disrupted by the wind, there were often false alarms.

TO: P

how could i have known it was a false alarm, growing into an open mouth despite the shudder of a full stomach, i'm sorry i gave you too much credit. i rlly thot i was dying

NEVER SENT

TO: K

i h8 that i'm praying to a god i don't believe in

NEVER SENT

TO: K

ur absence has taken root in my throat, i can feel its knot sucking my breath: a love story

NEVER SENT

"There is only one big thing — desire." In *The Song of the Lark*, Willa Cather, proven posthumously to have had lesbian relationships and also described as homophobic, calls the world little, its people little. "Human life is little," she adds.

TO: K

desire is a monstrous thing, it is a monstrous thing and maybe not the monster. look the first boy i kissed, kissed my hand too, for days on end, my hand was the first site of violence, i kept picking at it, a sternum opening. every night, at my mother's bedside, i said his name aloud till i was sick of it, i didn't want to go anywhere, i didn't want to go anywhere and thank fuck you left

NEVER SENT

TO: K

i read the texts you thot u deleted b4 i could read, i h8 that u think of me like that

NEVER SENT

She kept crying for Punnuh. Sassi could only take the weight of her own body but still stretched her arms in the desert. As if there was something to touch, hold and hunger over. She never stopped looking for his mouth to empty into.

TO: K

sometimes i want to insist that i never loved you but then i remember how i kept saying ur name over and again until submission, i kept saying ur name as if it was the only name i knew, a prayer to all the sober gods

NEVER SENT

TO: K

may all tears u made me cry bless me

NEVER SENT

"Fuck, I'd go to Mars," read one comment under the *Jezebel* article "The Furthest You've Traveled For Sex". In the Jiji Zarina Baloch's song, "Pere Pawandi Saan" —in English, "I will get on my feet." Sassi pleads with Punnuh to stay the night in Bhambore. I do not want to plead for love. But I'd go to Mars too. I say I do not want to plead for love and still I do.

I almost sent you the email: *Everything beautiful is in your image. And I cannot look away from you. I do not want to. Let me. Allow me. Honour me by honouring yourself. From here on out, I can only love you more. All the more.*

TO: K

i was wrong, i can look away and i should

NEVER SENT

"Ultimately, it is the desire, not the desired, that we love" (Friedrich Nietzsche). *And what does Nietzsche know of desire*, my friends argue. *What does anybody*, I ask.

TO: K

i offered u my mouth once, then the entire face: a love story

are you hungry? i asked: a love story

we hardly fucked that night: a love story

the next morning my mother called to ask me if i'm okay: a love story

i desired u in the most obvious, most simple way: a love story

i wish i didn't waste so much time wanting u: a love story

NEVER SENT

TO:
"सुनते हैं के मिल जाती है हर चीज़ दुआ से

इक रोज़ तुम्हें माँग के देखेंगे ख़ुदा से"

fuck me for thinking i ever wanted u: a love story

fuck me: a love story

DELETED FROM DRAFTS

TO:

Sirin Kale explains touch starvation: "It's why babies in neonatal intensive care units are placed on their parent's naked chests. It's the reason that prisoners in solitary confinement often report craving human contact as ferociously as they desire their liberty."

FROM DRAFTS

TO: K

if you do not hold me, i'm afraid I do not know what it means to be held.
i was the only witness to the stone kissing the river's breast headfirst.
everywhere i look today there's a ripple

DELETED FROM DRAFTS

TO:

i'm most afraid when no one's touching me or thinking of touching me

DELETED FROM DRAFTS

TO: K

ido not trust you to love me but i trust u to love

NEVER SENT

Punnuh cried *Sassi, Sassi* as he ran back to Bhambore. His voice scraped his own tongue hungry in a prayer, and when the ground shook and split open, he came so close and surrendered.

TO: K

lately all my prayers have been for u

i wish i could call u

TO: K

if u could'nt give me ur heart why pretend like you wanted to

now everytime i think abt u i'm disgusted with myself

i h8 that i'm still writing abt u

NEVER SENT

TO: K

i want to dickride ur feelings i want to jump off from the burning building into ur arms i want to be ur love interest not the placeholder until the one comes along, the internet calls me delusional and its fair, i'm going to burn in ur arms b4 i could burn at a stake

NEVER SENT

TO: K

i think i was trying to be a person i thot u wanted to love or could love if i practised hard enough, it's enough already, i don't have to be desperate, i don't have to be so beautiful

NEVER SENT

G.K Chesterton, an English philosopher and lay theologian, died of congestive heart failure at his home in Buckinghamshire. His last words were to his wife Frances. *Good morning*, he said.

TO: K

i wanted to cling to u like that, to dwarf in ur light, more than i wanted
to ask u abt ur day i wanted u to come to me and tell me all abt it, i wanted u to make me in ur memory the softest animal, most bountiful and
least hungry and i'm surprised to discover that u did, i'm disappointed
u could not smell the hunger rotting inside of me, i mourned a version
of reality where u see me how i want to be seen but not for what i am,
i'm supposed to be happy and i deceived u into believing i'm something
completely wonderful when only i'm just the most recent one in ur day

NEVER SENT

Mahmoud Darwish insists, "A University degree, four books and hundreds of articles and I still make mistakes when reading. You wrote me 'good morning' and I read it as 'I love you.'"

TO: K

i insisted that i love u and u insisted i didn't, i'm sorry that u feel so
unloveable at times, that u must project ur feelings of being unloveable
onto me and then come with explanations to rationalize those feelings,
i can only love u and i can only love u if u let me

NEVER SENT

Chesterton notes: "Love is not blind; that is the last thing that it is. Love is bound; and the more it is bound the less it is blind."

TO: K

i couldn't have been in love more than when you convinced me you couldn't love me and i loved you still and i said i would always love you and i suppose we were both indulging ourselves, we lied to each other: you chose not to love me and i didn't love you always

NEVER SENT

June 29, 2022 was the shortest day since the atomic clock was invented. The earth completed its rotation 1.59 milliseconds fast. There have been shorter days on earth, scientists insist.

TO: P

there has not been a shorter day on earth, i insisted when i was getting up to leave and u insisted i stay for another 10 minutes. insistence, i argued, is a particular brand of love. u insisted on buying me flowers, u insisted we could fuck if i wanted to and i didn't rlly want to and you said you were okay with it but i could see u were disappointed, i could see all the ways this could've gone badly in a different story but u insisted this was a love story and i wanted to reward ur patience with a first kiss, at the end of the year, u insisted u loved me and i insisted that i could never forget u and look i remember u more than allow myself to, look i didn't forget u, look i'm talking abt a love story and ur still alive in it

NEVER SENT

A common phrase on the passenger side mirrors in motor vehicles reads: "objects in (the) mirror appear closer than they are."

TO: P

i suppose i imagined u more beautiful than u are, it didn't occur to me then that i was looking at this world from in-between the hair of ur chest, i imagined u were more kind to me because i loved u, i imagined loving u more then, let me pretend u misinterpreted the safety warning as i did

NEVER SENT

TO: P

do not ask me abt my day: a safety warning

do not text me the first thing in the morning: a safety warning

do not eyefuck me: a safety warning

do not kiss me without trying to love me: a safety warning

do not fantasize abt me unless it's too sad and it must be done: a safety warning

do not lick my ass: a safety warning:

do not call me beautiful: a safety warning

NEVER SENT

TO:

Daguerre is believed to be the first person to take a photograph of the moon. Using his own process, which came to be known as daguerreo-type, he took a picture on January 2, 1839. But the picture was lost in a fire, a contemporary reported. A fire. Then the picture was deleted for everyone forever.

FROM DRAFTS

TO:

i miss you

DELETED FOR EVERYONE

Notes
I was inspired by Melissa Broder's essay "Help Me Not Be a Human Being" from her book
So Sad Today where she writes lines like "I never liked myself: a love story" and "When
you said you just wanted it to be a one-night thing, I kinda hoped you meant one night
over and over until we die: a love story" and many others.
Sassi Punnu is one of the seven popular tragic romances of Sindh.

FORGIVE ME FATHER I KNOW LOVE A TOUCH DIFFERENTLY AND IT TASTES SM BETTER WHEN MY LOVER KISSES ME AND I GET TO KISS HER BACK

THIS IS NOT A SIN BUT STILL I NEED SOMEONE I NEED SOMEONE TO TELL ME THEY SEE HOW TRULY SORRY I AM AND I AM SORRY FOR EVERYTHING THAT IS NOT IN MY CONTROL

AND I NEED SOMEONE TO HOLD MY FACE IN THEIR HANDS AND TELL ME THEY FORGIVE ME BEFORE THEY LOVE ME

OBITUARY FOR [REDACTED]

Admit it: you want their gender. That's not a secret anymore. Now you're here talking about how much trans lives matter, thank you for treating their funeral like a seminar presentation for your gender studies class. [Redacted] would've presented you with the best ally award except [Redacted] is dead, except you weren't really the ally when they needed you to be. [Redacted] didn't want to ruin the vibes so [Redacted] only talked to you about things that didn't almost kill them. Invite [Redacted] to your university as the first dead speaker. [Redacted] will miss you at your funeral. [Redacted] was never beautiful and you will never know that. [Redacted] could write more poems. [Redacted] is looking for a publisher. Tune in later for [Redacted's] book of poems about coming out as dead when you're trans.

THIS IS A CONFESSION

This is a terrible confession: A Twitter user describes Satoshi Kon's *Tokyo Godfathers*: "Rewatched Tokyo Godfathers by Satoshi Kon and it's so, so amazing. An extremely good Christmas movie!!!*** /   ***transphobia/homophobia aside," and I would agree with VoidBurger (AKA Jess) but I'm unable to put the transphobia aside. The fact is, I watched myself grieve my own house for months, its tripwire hung loose. My hands, refusing touch. My wrists, no longer cobalt blue. Everything was marked with a sign: *do not touch* and nobody did. I was angry because I was finally alone and not in the way I had imagined I wanted to be, not at a writing retreat in a foreign city where the French want to fuck me and jazz plays in the background. I was alone in my house and the city and everybody in it felt like one big stranger to me, including her.

This is the confession that makes everything hurt more: She was the first girl I loved after my mother. The audience insisted we were two sisters and it wasn't exactly untrue. But it wasn't that, either, and I never complained. She was a year older than me and for the larger part of my childhood I was taller than her. I don't really remember at what point she stood bigger than me. Loving her was good and bush-fire warm. The safe childhood I didn't have feels like a mistake when I'm holding her hand. I'm holding her hands in Chandigarh and Jagraon and all the places between. She was my *almost*, then.

This is an understated confession: But that's the other thing about what is *almost*. You either have it or you don't. And now somehow you're in that liminal space, glowing with uncertainty and the proof of life. You've either touched it or you've not. You've either kissed her or it's a dream still in the summer afternoon. Whatever is *almost* bends all the laws of physics. You're nearly there. *Nearly*: that's the keyword. I'm near her but not quite.

This is the confession I'm most proud to make: It feels wrong to use that word. *Obsessed*. But I can see how someone would use it to describe a crush. It borders obsession. It can be love in all its consuming ways. But I don't intend to write a treatise on love and I'm not too proud to wear my heart on my sleeve. Especially on days like these when I'm reminded of her as I scroll endlessly through my phone. Standing in the kitchen I take the mango in my hand and pull its skin off. I'm gentle with every beast and every fruit. Last night in an almost-dream my dadi cut me up some mango and I ate it with the roti. I know love by what it does to me. I want to eat my own head and understand how my desire preserves me. I think I'm falling in love again and I'm not too proud to wear my heart on my sleeve. I wear it nonetheless.

This is a confession I want to give up claim to: Five summers ago we were still holding hands. We were friends, too. I remember cooking up an omelet for her in the kitchen and she cooked me some maggi. At the dinner table we were grateful for each other. When we slept next to each other we shared all our secrets. I knew the girl in the neighbourhood she disliked but I never understood why and I don't remember her answer when I asked her. I loved sitting behind her when she rode the bicycle even when I wanted a chance to ride it alone.

This is the confession to writing about it all: When I think about her today I feel sad. I feel like time did us wrong. I feel like I was betrayed by forces greater than me. I don't even dream of her and here I am dreaming of a world where she comes around eventually. Where we speak to each other and she will hold my hand again before I even ask her to hold mine. I did not tell anybody I loved her. This is my punishment and I know I have suffered enough. I have seen her, too. I remember the night she cried to me in bed. She was scared she was going to flunk in her maths exam. We both prayed together. She prayed that she'd pass the exam and I prayed that she'd wake up with news even better than she had hoped for. I mean who was I even praying to in heaven. I mean when the lights went out and we lit candles in the house I remember trying to scare her as a joke and it was funny then. I mean we were both in the same room and it couldn't have been anybody else. For the first time in my life I knew what it was like to have a friend.

This is a small confession about my limitless loneliness: I didn't have friends before. I hate to admit but I was that kid in school who sat and ate their lunch alone. I would sketch in my notebook and sing outside the library. A boy I liked once saw me scribble "I want to die" on the desk and I spent a good fifteen minutes trying to erase it later. I mean I did want to die and didn't want to die. I mean I *almost* wanted to die then.

This is the confession everybody remembers: Death didn't seem so cruel then. I remember the day she told the principal at her school that she had to leave soon because her great grandfather died. He was still alive then. She wanted to come home early that day and hang out with me I know. I never took a day off and now I wish I had. I wish I had spent an extra day with her instead of spending time at school. I wished I had to never look up at the moon because she was there sitting next to me.

This is the first confession: I mean, I loved her. The last time I saw her we only exchanged pleasantries. I wanted to say more. I know and she wanted to say more, too—or so I imagine at my worst, and hope at my best.

This is the confession where I first make note of the fact she loved me: She was always proud of me and I wonder where we went wrong. She would introduce me to her friends: *she is like the smartest at her school.* I probably was, too, I'd like to think, but that's irrelevant now. All I am trying to remember now is her voice. All I will argue for is this: you should've heard her then. If you had heard her, you would've known that she loved me, too.

This is a confession about being right: I thought I made peace with our fallout. I thought perhaps with time I would forget about you. But it keeps coming back like the sun. It was a summer afternoon again. We were in the park and I pointed you towards the lemon tree in someone's garden. You filled the red basket I brought from my house with their lemons and then the aunty in the next house saw us. She took the basket from your hands and we went back to my house. I thought I never wanted to show my face again. But I was wrong then, and I'm hoping I'm wrong now.

This is a confession that I miss summers and for the reasons you think I do: At my house, we danced together. I didn't think I loved dancing so much and I don't think I had ever seen a more graceful dancer than her. Part of it is the fact that she danced well and enjoyed it too. But most of it is love I know now and I'm not saying love makes us blind. Love only makes us in the image of the animal we run towards.

I'm not an expert in love and even if I was I could never carry the weight of the title. I know I make a fool of the time I give to the world freely. I know I have kissed enough and am a fool to still want the lime juice that soured me. I mean I loved her and that was time. I mean the summers I spent at her house were my favourite. I don't think I could ever think of summer and not think of her. Her hand on my face trying to wake me up in the morning. Her hand holding my hand as we walk through the sector market. Her hand pointing us in the direction of whatever still I would love less than her.

This is not the confession you think it is: I loved her and I joked about kissing her and it was only a joke. This sentence though reminds me of that one porn title, *I'm not a lesbian but...* and I'm not trying to beat the gay allegations. But that aside, we kissed on accident one or two times. I mean she reached in to kiss my cheek and I turned my face towards her. I mean I'm no longer sure who was my first kiss anymore. Her or the girl at my school I was friends with and kissed in the play-ground. I mean I don't think whatever accident this was counts as a kiss. I mean I don't think I would've hated it even if it was. It was a joke and it was a lovely one too if we can both laugh at the end of it and we did then.

This is a confession, not a joke: Being queer isn't that joke when your parents are ashamed of your queerness. Being queer isn't that joke when my parents insist that I remove my pronouns from my WhatsApp bio. Or when I come out to a friend and she asks if I want to fuck her now. Or when I come out to another friend and she says *that's cool and all but I'm not into you like that.* Being queer isn't that joke when strangers on Twitter slide into my DMs to ask me about my genitals. Or when my parents bring up conversion therapy. Or when my psychiatrist told my mother that it was a phase I will grow out of and perhaps even a trend among the kids to pass off as cool. Whatever the fuck she means. It makes me want to die for good and not almost die and I say it sincerely. Being queer isn't the joke you think it is when my father switches the channel when a trans person is speaking and calls it all nonsense. I'm too scared to even use the word gay around the house, afraid what it might bring. I'm afraid my father will scream at me again or threaten to beat me up. I'm afraid I must delete every poem and every text from a friend that knows I'm queer and I'm unhappy when I'm at home or in the world. Being queer is never that joke you think it is.

This is my least favourite confession: I mean I loved her. I loved her for so long and I heard the word from her first and she said it with contempt or what sounds like disgust. I mean I heard her say the word and it made me wonder if I should run and hide from it. Her voice then was so different from all her other voices. I didn't think of it then but it still made me uncomfortable. *Gay*. She said it like it was a bad word. I mean I know that because I once said it too like that later in school. I mean whatever internalised homophobia that was. I mean I'm still scared of her. I mean much later I realised she was homophobic too.

This is a confession of love, not a love confession: It is another summer night and we are still sitting in the park and I'm trying to tell her that I'm not straight or cisgender. But she says something and it sounds like dissolution. I don't know how she did it but she made it sound like being queer was atrocious and it wasn't hilarious one bit and I laughed and then I was laughing in my own face. It was that moment I knew that if I told her I was not a girl or even straight she would stop talking to me. I know she would have distanced from me. More than the distance she had already built unintentionally and I could live with that. I could live with this distance. I could live in the moment where she doesn't know she is closing the door because she hasn't seen me. It is harder to live where she looks me in the eye and then she closes the door in my face. I mean I could never come out to her after that and I tried. I mean I once said I love you and at the same time I could never use the words *I* or *love* or *you*.

This is the confession that tries to piece it all together unsuccessfully: I don't know what happened then but I could guess. I mean that summer my father tells me that she had told him that I once said I wanted to have sex with her and I cried to my mother in bed *why would she say that about me?* I mean my father told me that someone sent her my nudes and then she told them everything about me and I still don't know what that *everything* is but she looked me up online after. All I know is that that summer my relatives had seen my nudes on the internet and they had read my posts where I had come out as trans and queer and this took place right after she told them I had blocked her on my social media. I made my social media accounts private but then I received a follow request from an account that I'm sure was her father's. I mean I never wanted her to find me on the internet and look at me like that, like she had just discovered tragedy but only knew how to laugh. I wanted to keep that part separate from her and everybody else in my family. She said what she said and we never spoke again.

This is not a confession I'm making at a family event unless I'm drunk to all my wit's end: I couldn't catch my weight. I put my arm around myself, how a child hugs the empty space. My brows didn't furrow. My heartbeat still slowed down in an effort to contain itself. It was so quiet, I dreaded it. Even the tiny beast of my body could not put the blood back into the earth. If there was one thing I understood, it was this: there was no coming back. All these years of friendship, all the time, whether enough or not, is still time spent together and I wanted to go to her house so many times in the night and scream: *You're terrible. You're terrible. How could you do that to me? I'm so sorry, I miss you. I miss you so much. Please talk to me.*

This is a confession about the colour red: Whatever was left unsaid was left to its own devices. If language alone could pull the body ashore, it would've done weeks ago, centuries before, maybe at the beginning of time too. But there was little it could do to mend what was broken or breaking apart, slowly for us. I knew deep down that even when both she and I described love in the same language, used the same descriptors, they still meant different things. Language is a response to the world, not the world. Wittgenstein, in his treatise on colour, asked, "Can't we imagine certain people having a different geometry of colour than we do?" I agree that red is a beautiful colour for a basket.

This is a confession I make to everybody else and not the person for whom it is intended: I agree that continuing to swipe on Hinge out of a habit I built out of loneliness is not a good look. I mean, frankly, I'm not all that interested in the couple looking for a unicorn or the man who breaks the conversation with, "You look super FH. Hope you know what FH means." I don't care and I do care. I spend hours internet sleuthing and it's a waste. According to one of the many Urban Dictionary definitions, FH is an acronym for "Forgotten Hope," a popular realism modification for the computer game *Battlefield 1942*. "Forgotten hope," I never say it. I'm not a nihilist and I don't intend to be one, not at least when I'm sober. So I say it to my mother: *I miss her*.

This is a confession that I'm too scared to make: I miss her like it was a Tuesday on a summer afternoon and we had just come back with that red basket full of lemons and no one saw us or caught us. I miss

98

her in the park sitting on that bench thinking we have come here for a picnic and we have come here for a picnic. We have arrived in every park before the moon could ever arrive. We were the sailors of the summer night and there is so much I wanted to share with her. I wanted to tell her about the first boy I had kissed at nineteen. I wanted to tell her about my new crush and how obsessive I feel and how much in love I could soon, very potentially, very possibly be. I wanted to tell her about the flowers this boy sent to my address in Delhi. I wanted to tell her about the time I had sex with this boy I loved and his mother called and he never stopped, not once, speaking to her. I miss her like a terribly important detail in a story I must revise. I miss her like a terribly unimportant detail in a story I'm fixating on but shouldn't.

This is not a confession of resentment: I don't know whether I am hungry or if it's simply the beating of my own heart, a relentless pursuit. Sometimes, when the video buffers and the screen goes black and I look at myself, I am overcome with a feeling: I want to be flung into the deepest recesses of the ocean or maybe the pit of my own stomach. I do not know which one it is that I'm more scared of: the unexplored, the known, or the mutable hunger that I've stumbled over my whole life, the hunger that rots inside me. Resentment: that was the final mark of our love.

This is the confession you think it is: I'm convinced memory is a parasite of the body. I miss her terribly. It sounds like a joke when I say it: all that homophobia aside, she was my favourite cousin and we don't get too many favourite cousins if we're not lucky. I never had another favourite cousin after her. She will come around, I hope. Eventually, we will speak. Eventually, we will hold hands and maybe she won't think of me in the same words she uses to describe something atrocious. I keep telling myself this like a mantra these days.

This is the sincerest confession out of all the rest: I don't know anymore and it's been too long. I'm not a girl or straight and it's okay to assume maybe she knows now but it's not okay with me that we haven't spoken since. I knew that and still didn't. I almost know this pain and if it meant that I could spend another day with her, who knows I might briefly be a girl in that world again.

*FATHER LOOK AT ME FATHER I AM STILL YOUR
CHILD AND YOU ARE STILL MY FATHER AND
I WANT TO BE INVINCIBLE AND I CANNOT
CHANGE HISTORY FATHER WON'T YOU LOOK
AT ME ONCE*

I'M STILL HERE

HOROSCOPE FOR FRIDAY

Dear Sagittarius,

When he hugs you so completely, you imagine you dissolve. In a world where he touches you again, you're lucky if you're alive. Slowly and surely you become your body; under the lights he kisses you. The street is a bushfire and you're drowning in his direction. One of the earliest Roentgen's x-ray prints feature his wife Bertha's hand with her wedding ring. "I have seen my death," she exclaimed, after undergoing the world's first x-ray. *I have seen my death*, you whisper under your breath when he kisses you for the first time. Because you have seen your death, you have also seen what you imagined couldn't kill you until the end. You witness whatever is beautiful happen to you like an accident across the road. You imagine you are helpless in what he does to you.

WATER MEMORY

Mahiwal died in Chenab. I watched him dissolve for hours into the night sky, his body floating in the wraps of the Milky Way. He was unremarkable in bed, his lungs were sorry, hands chapped and small. He cupped Sohni's face into his palms. He carried her memory like a butcher's knife, full with hunger. One night, his body lunged towards the riverbed, chasing Sohni's reflection. A reflection is, after all, a memory without witness. *After all.*

&

I'm the only witness to my father's shroud. I do not remember him like I used to. In my memory, he is small, a static child in a wastebasket, spring suspended inside the empty spaces between my fingers. I could've pulled him out, stretched him thin on the film screen. I could've kissed his hands too. My right cheek is still sore.

&

Science says our earliest memories are older than we think. At two and a half, I think, I could've learnt to love the sound the firecrackers made against the drowning of stars in the sky but instead I feared them. Like how I fear dogs when they bark, the ambulance siren loud in its despair, breathless lungs, cold shoulders.

&

My memories hold what I cannot. Is it still a memory if I can't remember it.

&

"These memories of love are malleable," says Lawrence Patihis, a researcher at the University of Southern Mississippi. Is there, ever, an objective way to love someone? Could I love you without me?

&

When I was small, I ran away from the house. Mostly, I ran away from my father. I ran so fast, my guts spilled onto the park benches. The ground hot pink with my blood. *Father, can you hear me?*

&

My memory is a sick child, running from one end of the park to another. My memory is the stretch between the places we want to go for each other but cannot.

&

I had loved him without my remembering and without his reminding. I like the part where we think to surrender is annihilation and mistake the thunder for the sound of rain. Sohni died in the arms of the river. She reached for Mahiwal's hands but could only grab fistfuls of water. Like Sohni, I reached for my father's hands and latched onto the bruised air, thick between our silken prayers. There is no memory of death, only dissolution.

&

Both the sound and the light vibrate and become known to us in a fraction of seconds. Do we, then, love the colour more or the sound? When I close my eyes shut, I can no longer listen either. This is how I remember.

&

Anyone who has ever been in love will remember the memory, however sacred and ugly. So sometimes, I wonder: was I in love with the boy, or his memory, when his ugly hands, for the first time, held my ugly face, arrow-shaped, pointing towards the lanterns in the sky?

&

Did Sohni love Mahiwal or was he just someone she remembered without failing?

&

In 1988, Jacques Benveniste published a study in the international scientific journal *Nature*, in which he claimed that water "remembered" previously dissolved substances even after they were gone. I do not care if this contradicts our understanding of physical chemistry. All I know is that even after Sohni and Mahiwal drowned, their voices called to each other from under the river. All I know is that Chenab cannot sleep or stop with the memory of dying in its folds forever flowing.

&

"Because I could not stop for Death," Emily Dickinson wrote. Then Anne Sexton wrote in her poem, "Since you ask, most days I cannot remember." My heart is insistent and detectable. I simply want and I'm shameless for the things I want. When I'm sleeping next to my father, I want to be less like him. *For you, I will never be my father*, I told the first girl I fell in love with and then kissed her hands in the parking lot. In the evening, I pull my ribs out and learn to make a stringed instrument at home. Music can kill us, too.

&

Mozart died while writing *Requiem*, a requiem mass for the dead. Symphony No.6, *Pathetique*, is considered Tchaikovsky's musical suicide note. When Puccini visited Tuscanini, he begged "Don't let my *Turandot* die." Once, when I was listening to music, I chose to drown in the bathtub. I didn't come up for air or call for help, I stationed my body into stillness and muffled cries.

&

I hear my father cry over the phone when he asks me to return but he doesn't mention anything about home. *Return where*, I ask myself. *Pray to god*, he keeps telling me. I want to tell him that this is not how this works but instead I sew my mouth with nails, pressing my lips against each other. How else do I know I'm here? The next morning when he calls, I tell him I'm okay instead and ask how he is. He says he is okay, too, and I can't believe we are so much like each other. When he isn't sad, he is always angry, so I stop answering his calls.

&

The only way I know how to be a good daughter is by marrying the despair my father knocks over on the kitchen slab. I have heard him say it enough times: ਮਾਂ ਪਿਓ ਦੀਆਂ ਗਾਲਾਂ, ਪਿਓ ਦੀਆਂ ਨਾਲਾਂ. This is his way of saying that he means well, even when he is hurting me. That I'm ungrateful. That I could be wretched, wet in blue paint, I could be dead like the wave that ran over the shore and retreated.

&

I, shameless creature of the Chenab, earthenware wicked, brought him shame, and shame must go.

&

My father, beautiful earth man. Of course, he saw disobedience as a sign that we didn't love him anymore. It becomes increasingly hard to nurse a suspicious heart. Of course, we were lonely with each other.

&

Fear is a learned memory. I hide all the water in the house inside bottles. Water poisoning is the disruption of brain function due to drinking too much water and it is potentially fatal. I'm convinced everything is killing me. Paper cuts hurt bad, but no one died from a paper cut, except those who did, like the man who contracted a gruesome flesh-eating bug from a paper cut. The newspaper tells about a man who died in his sleep. I can't be too cautious.

&

If the human body is 70 percent water and water we know remembers, can we then also say the body is 70 percent of memories? I close my eyes and all I can do is remember. All this remembrance rings in my ears until I bleed. I hate this red.

&

Memories can kill us, too. They are the ghosts that orbit our body. I could not look away anymore.

&

When Sohni bites into Mahiwal's carved thigh thinking it's fish that she's eating, she forgets. How can she remember what she doesn't know?

&

I do not care if my father apologizes, I care if he remembers. I want him to remember.

&

Nothing happened instantaneously. I know.

I know he didn't wake up that day thinking he wanted to hurt me. Danielle Sered says somewhere: *no one experiences harm for the first time when they do harm.* I think about it every morning, just before breakfast, my hands full with grief, naming every animal a beast, every beast my love.

&

When we withdraw love, do we withdraw love from the person or the memory?

&

Sometimes I think I chased my own reflection, not Mahiwal's, and drowned.

Notes
Sohni Mahiwal is one of the four popular tragic romances of Punjab. Both Sohni and Mahiwal drowned in Chenab.

HOROSCOPE FOR SATURDAY

Dear Sagittarius,

Your father is a stubborn goat on a hill. He needed you to know that blood is thicker than water, that blood clots at the site of the wound to prevent it from bleeding too much. You are a stubborn horse in the open fields and you only needed your father to know summer like you did, from a good distance, a safe distance, summer dislodged from the nape of your neck, all under-ripe mangoes & a child buried under debris. You were small then & now you must enjoy the red stain on your face, the wind blowing in the direction your imaginary penis swings in your sweet dreams. You must celebrate the cartilage that bends over and over but does not break, not like the bone. You never imagined your brother knew before you came out to everybody else but then he said he always did, he always did.

THE QUEER QUEST

an interactive nonfiction game about struggles with transphobia at home and school

after *Depression Quest*

WELCOME

This is an interactive game where you are met with multiple choices. The goal is to understand transphobia and present as real a simulation. This is but one representation that may or may not be shared by all users.

Many of us don't have the same luxuries as others. Many people experiencing transphobia and abuse in their homes cannot seek the support they need. This could be for a variety of reasons. Sometimes it's having no financial means to access the kind of help we want or perceived stigma behind navigating ties with one's family. You are called selfish to want to sever ties if you so choose. You are the ungrateful child if you decide you even want to address it.

This game attempts to veer with that understanding. You might not share these experiences and that's okay. This game is an entry point to an experience, both devastating and, sadly, common.

Thank you for playing.

BEGIN

It's a year before high school ends. You are sitting next to a girl who is your friend, who you think is your friend, that is your consolation.

Memory invites you to reimagine your world as either safer or crueler. Tonight you've chosen to rest under the first shade of the tree. You're young and sweet and you're seventeen. The magic of the dancing queen that ABBA had you believing you were is missing and you laugh with your mouth open. Wherever you dance among your friends, your body is the first outline in the crowd. From a distance, everything looks fine, but when you step closer, all edges and lines drawn in chalk are smudged.

NEXT

You've known for a while now. You are the frightening thing in your mother's mouth. She jokes around asking if you're gay. *What makes you think*—you begin, slipping the question. You only liked the girls because they looked nice, you insist. You were always friends with them, you insist. They were kind to you, you insist. What other reason do you need to like someone, you insist. It's the same everywhere, you insist. I'm sure you liked your friends too, you insist, and your mother listens without paying attention to the pages you've dogeared. All these pages celebrating a resignation of girlhood and heterosexuality. Nobody knows that. Nobody needs to know that, you insist one final time.

NEXT

You're walking back from school. You remember the words your friend passed to you. How they arrived in a flash without a token of understanding. Now all your system's devices bug you into submission.

Your friend has noted: *that's such a Tumblr thing*. You were talking about gender neutral pronouns and she started on woke culture. You realise that maybe today is not the right time to come out to her as trans. You reach home to find everything where you left it. You are no longer a witness to your heart, now culpable to all that you're pained into doing.

You relegate to default settings and here you are nursing your wound into another. You want one true kiss and neither *gender non-confirming* nor *homosexuality* are the buzzwords your friend thinks they are.

NEXT

You're at school, under the sun, all thick with insurmountable solitude. Your friends embrace you. You like coming to school to see them. The lunch break is over and you're back in your class. You're sitting next to a girl and listening to her treatise on bisexuality. *I think I'm bisexual*, you say, and she insists that you're not. *You're like straight and my gaydar is incredibly strong*, she adds. You do not even want to process what this means. You only want to hide in your bed. You think you'd like to perform bisexuality. You're desperate to be recognised by a straight girl and her gaydar.

WHAT DO YOU DO?

A.   **You insist that you're queer as fuck.**
B.   **You agree that you're straight.**

You've chosen Option A.
Your fate rests on a random subatomic event. This is the event. You saw this coming and you didn't see this coming. Maybe this is Schrodinger's cat.

Your friend makes three observations based on your confession:
1.   Does this mean you're attracted to me, then?
2.   Were you flirting with me, I should've known you were flirting with me.
3.   I just want to make it very clear that I'm straight by the way.

You're still friends with her, and at the same time, not friends with her anymore. This is the real Schrodinger's cat. This is what you wish someone had prepared you for. You wish time travel was real and you could take your confession back. You know that going back in time would've changed nothing.

You've chosen Option B.
You feel uncomfortable when she insists on heterosexuality. There's no convincing a straight person. You stop right there. You make a face she isn't looking at and you say *you're right.*

Congratulations! You're straight now.

Being biromantic is your new consolation prize. You want to forget that you even brought it up. Your friend doesn't say much and you're grateful for the silence you share as it chokes you a little at first, and then all of sudden.

NEXT

You're eighteen and you never use the word *gay* at home. If somebody brings it up, you pretend you didn't hear it. *Gay, what's that?* You pretend your body into believing that you have no occasion to use the word. The utterance amounts to confession, you believe. Maybe that's partly true in your case. Your father makes a homophobic joke in the same vein as one you laughed at three years back. It's not okay, except you're willing to give yourself the benefit of the doubt and not him. Except you afford yourself the compassion that you do not offer him. Except you cannot be homophobic because you're gay and he is not. That is all bullshit and you know it. You are afraid to look at yourself in the mirror. You're afraid to recognise all the ways in which you've faltered, too. You try to make amends. You offer a prayer in the middle of the night to whatever gods might be listening, however straight. You wish your father a good morning when you wake up and you allow yourself to call him your father. You allow yourself to love him one more time, always one more time.

NEXT

You've forgiven people even though you have no power to forgive anybody. How do you even forgive someone for anything at all if you never stop looking at the mirror? Your cousin marked queerness in colours so bright and blue you cannot look away without trying to assemble your body outside of all the blue in the world. You're gay and now it's the saddest blue you've seen and you cannot be sad or blue and least of all gay. You cannot be gay if you must be loved in ways you want to be loved, you're convinced, and that's sad. It's such a sad thing. You try one more time and you tell your cousin that it's okay to like girls and she takes this as a confession.

NEXT

You do not know what a confession is except only you've offered a bunch of them in passing. You'd never thought your parents would look you up on the internet and they do. They found your pictures. Your body under the lights, dim and unconvincing. You slept with men for money and you did not keep it a secret from the world, not Twitter at least. You shouldn't have to but who's going to explain to your parents. You touch your arm in vain, offer a shy smile to the person in the mirror. You think it isn't so terrible but then it hits you how your uncle has sent you a follow request. How your aunts only knew your face by your body and its way to aperture, in the lights in your father's room, you're all mouth and tenuous.

NEXT

Your father wants to talk to your cousin again. Your father keeps asking you to delete the pronouns from your bio and you do. He asks you to stop calling yourself trans and you pretend to walk back into your closet. He makes you feel like how your mother feels. She said she disliked your father but she loves him. You want to return back into all your photographs and return the clothes. You want to kiss yourself less and you want to surrender your arms. Your hands wave an outline and signal desperation into the air. Your parents take away your phone and your laptop and you watch your own life like a magic show. The joke does not get as many laughs as you think it would.

WHAT DO YOU DO?

A. You tell your parents that you'll leave.
B. You tell your parents that you won't mention to anyone you're
  queer.

You've chosen Option B.
You know life is not worth the pain you're writing yourself in. You know you'd rather tear your lungs apart. You'd rather offer your liver to an animal god to change the outcome. You thought you'd forget the summer like a breeze but it keeps hitting you in the face. You're home and nowhere.

You've chosen Option A.
You're afraid that if you leave right now, you'll never be able to return. You want to return not because you think this is home but because you think this is the place between home and the strange city. If you've not found home, you have a place to rest here and now you have to leave. You don't have money and you have no place to stay and Delhi is the closest and the farthest place from Chandigarh. It doesn't matter whether you stay or not, you know you'll die either way.

THINK YOU MIGHT WANT TO QUIT?

PRESS CTRL + S TO SAVE.

PRESS CTRL + Z TO UNDO YOUR ACTIONS.

THANK YOU FOR PLAYING THE GAME.

IF YOU COULD LOOK AT YOUR FATHER AGAIN

*LOOK AT YOUR FATHER AGAIN HE IS NOT A
MONSTER AND NEITHER ARE YOU*

HE IS NOT INNOCENT AND NEITHER ARE YOU

*THIS IS A SYMPTOM OF BEING ALIVE SO YOU
MUST TAKE THIS HUNGER AND KISS IT*

KISS IT OVER AND OVER AND OVER

DO NOT STOP UNTIL YOU'RE FULL

HOROSCOPE FOR SUNDAY

Dear Sagittarius,

If in the stories that you write about your family you never write about my brother, then he doesn't exist. You weren't trying to be cruel, you weren't a vengeful little god, you didn't wrap your teeth against his soft body for bone. You only stood under the neem tree you imagined your father planted and watched your brother cry. It wasn't the first time and if you're lucky, it won't be the last, either. Nobody saw you swap your drink for his, you wanted to taste what was in his glass, it was sweet and his glass was bigger. You had every reason to blame each other for your misfortunes but bless you you didn't. Bless the summer you picked the lemons, the juiciest, from the neighbour's backyard, lemons you stole, but you didn't call it that back then.

THREE SELF-PORTRAITS
WITH A PRAYER

I. SELF-PORTRAIT WITH A PRAYER DISGUISED AS A MEDITATIVE STUDY ON THE FATHER-DAUGHTER RELATIONSHIP

My father was preparing dinner in the kitchen, I thought it was a little early for that. I made him tea while he was cutting up the pomegranate, later. It was a summer like any other. I had no rules, no gloss on my lips, my hair was neatly oiled into a plait. Summer, I thought, was the most forgiving season. I let summer run its course, year after year. I saw the first summer of a childhood that I never had. It was beautiful and now the word feels shallow and ugly in my mouth. God, I'm afraid to call anything beautiful anymore. If it isn't, in two words, real and tangible, it begins to feel like pain or its memory. I have grown up inside the body of the season where familial love takes the shape of the hand of a bigger animal and you're somewhere down the food chain and you're running in circles because that's what a forest is. I never thought of it like that until summer dislodged itself from the nape of my neck. I could finally see my father and his hands were so much bigger than mine and they held my hands too. God, maybe summer was never real, it could've been winter after all, with its cold antics and lucky charms. The ridiculous thing about lucky charms isn't that they're lucky or that we believe they are lucky. I think what makes them ridiculous is that we'd keep finding lucky charm after lucky charm. There was always another summer and I felt bitter with what I thought I was doing and I was afraid that whether my father was wrong or not, I would've found reasons to dislike him. But that fear was the last symptom of summer, it wasn't true or real. I was permitted to never show my face. I was asked to leave the house in the middle of the night again. He said I should kill myself or he would kill me. He threatened to beat me up because I spoke out of turn. God, does he know that I cover my face when I laugh, that when my lover told me I look a little like my father, I cried, and when my lover explained "only the good parts," I cried harder. God, I want to see the good parts too, not remember them from a nursery rhyme. God, I never speak out of turn and I apologise when I whisper. I'm trying to remember the last time my father held me and I wasn't scared of him and instead, I remember dadi, she was sitting on the sofa for what felt like an awfully long hour. She fell asleep sitting down and I thought she was dead because she looked so calm. That evening, when she woke up finally, she pulled me into the kitchen, wrapped her small arm around my shoulders. For the first couple of minutes, it felt like a game. She was pointing to the obvious: *you're the eldest child. You're growing up, you'll have more responsibilities. You should take care of your father, learn to help around in the kitchen. You're the daughter of the house. You are your father's daughter.* The last one, it didn't register the same as the others. I am my father's daughter, yes. But I think in emphasizing that I was his daughter, everybody forgot the first fact, the very reason for that second fact: that he was my father before. He was my father before I was ever anything else.

II. SELF-PORTRAIT WITH A PRAYER FOR MY BROTHER'S LONG LIFE, HYDRATED SKIN, AND A LIFE WITH MY FRIENDS WHO ASK ME ABOUT MY DAY

I have never named my abusers. I'm not doing it today either. I'm not going to hold them hostage in an essay. I have only ever named my friends, I think, like that, with the urgency to mend a broken heart, at a pier, outside in the rain, when the lights have just gone out. God, I'm pathetic and I am desperate for the light at the end of the tunnel to choke me, leaving only trails of apologies offered in the wake. I do not ask for forgiveness, except when I run away and my body is lowered into the ground. I have never believed in god. But I thanked him for my misfortunes every night before going to bed. Yes, I counted others' blessings. Yes, I stood naked before the mirror and felt the enormous gaze of the body I kept with me. I don't know about you but I have wanted to erase a scar with a scar and I picked the knife and I measured in good faith the enormity of my desire. God, love isn't a terrible thing. But you won't try it. I'm sleeping next to my friend and I'm telling him this. The love and the lover aren't the same and yet when my lover walked through the door, the only words in my mouth were: *oh god, my love*. God, I just desperately needed someone to offer me a hand and ask: *how are you? I'm good*, I want to say. I practice it in my head every day too. At this rate, I'll be a professional by the end of my life. On the phone, it was always my father offering me that courtesy and we both knew it was more than that. His proud child. His proud pain. His proud concern. It dissolved into one. The part I do not like is: that I understand him and I wish I didn't. Because if I understand and I'm still angry I'm afraid it only speaks about my own failures. I have forgiven my father until I see him again. I am trying to forgive myself too in bed with my friend who touches me when I do not want to be touched, who hears a *yes* when I'm quiet and asleep. I was crying in the room but he couldn't hear me with his face lodged against my chest. I was crying because I was desperate for someone to offer that courtesy to me then, for someone to ask me how I'm doing in that moment, for the opportunity to say *I'm fine, thank you. Remnants of medications are often excreted into saliva, that's why antibiotics leave a bitter taste in the mouth*, my friend explains over text. God, I'm bitter in the morning when this friend asks if I'm okay and I think it's a little too late for that. I'm bitter when he is leaving because he hasn't left already. God, I'm choking on my own spit. In the morning, on my way to class, I imagine my brother died and I'm at his funeral and Noisettes' "Never Forget You" is playing on the radio and now I'm crying in the metro. This is the ridiculous lucky charm. I'm looking for reasons to grieve so I do not have to tend to what is at the heart of it all. God, I don't want to have to grieve another friendship lost. God, every time I have written about someone they left or didn't touch without hurting me or didn't touch me at all. My mother draws a line with her fingernail, pointed and sharp, into my arm. She tells me my skin needs some moisturizing. I'm hungry, yes, for touch. God, the men I loved hurt me. God, is it okay to call all my abusers friends? I'm afraid I don't know what I might do if I name the animal before I name the pain.

III. SELF-PORTRAIT AS A PRAYER TO MY FATHER WHO I HAVE REFERRED TO AS GOD IN THIS ESSAY AND THE OTHERS BECAUSE I WANT TO SPEAK TO HIM WITHOUT SPEAKING TO HIM

The body is not the only proof. Look what desire does to me even before it has done it. Even before my arms open up, wide, in agony, god, I'm anchored to the bottom and I cannot reach the surface for trying to reach you. God, I'm afraid you will answer my call for help with turning away again. God, if you're not looking at me, I feel I must be the most wretched creature on earth. If a lover says I am in fact beautiful, I must still come to terms with the fact that this body is mine. I'm moaning in my loneliness. God, I cannot talk about desire without talking about loneliness. God, if you love me, I think I have a reason to love myself. God, I just want you to love me back. In my dream house, there's a small fence and I thought it meant something important to the both of us. But God, maybe the fence represents nothing but the fence. These are the nights I want to kill myself. I reach to touch you and find only myself in the room, the walls you painted with these lines. God, my longing fills me up endlessly and I worry I have nothing to offer you but the person I am in death. God, I'm too old to live with shame so I live with my anger these days. Please don't ask me god what's on my mind, I'm afraid I will tell you and won't shut up. God, I'm scared of men but I'm more scared to be lonely. I have many times walked into the arms of men who I know will hurt me. God, please don't kill me. God, I hate being afraid of you. God, please stop crying. I can't hate you when you're crying.

PARTING GIFT

Loona is grieving Pooran's death. This is the final scene. I watch as I pull my body out of the bed and I'm relieved that I'm hungry. I'm shamelessly hungry and alive. This is the final scene and I have never been more scared of the bottom of the ocean floor, the marine debris, crashing cars, the roads splitting in two like breakfast fruit my father cuts me, and my hands move above my head in a prayer.

&

Because I have wanted to die I am scared when others share that they do, too. And so many times I have pulled the memory around my neck to keep my hands from choking. If I don't stop now, who else might ruin me.

&

A friend asked me: *why did I rush to see another man in the rain*. Another reminded me that I had to stop mothering men. But it's not like that. This act of reaching out to hold a hand is emblematic of how our own parents have held ours and I see their worries too. A friend tells me they want to die and I'm worried each time. Each time my hand goes into my pocket looking for something to hold onto but I find nothing except a stolen prayer.

&

When my partner on a phone call tells me they want to die too, I do not know what to tell them. I'm scared to say the wrong things so I mumble and nod and say "yeah" over and over. I need them to know I'm here. I need them to know it's winter and that I'm making the bed warm, so they should come home now.

&

My mother comes home from the office early one afternoon. Her wrist is bandaged and I'm in the bathroom washing the blood off her phone case. My hands do not stop shaking for days after. The knowledge that she wanted to die was terrible enough. I kept asking her why even when I perfectly understood. My voice broke with every syllable until it was nothing but static between us.

&

I have never understood why anybody would hold onto anger. Until one evening my mother sends me pictures, pictures dadi had left for me. I crooned dadi's name in the gold that dangles from her ears. It is wrong, I'm wrong, but I'm also angry. She should have been here and I was angry that she was gone. I do not remember our last conversation. Did I forget her if I never dreamt of her or of her sister? Dadi's sister looked nothing like her, though neither of them were beautiful to begin with and I was still angry because like them I was ugly in my own hands. I don't think anybody quite understands what it means to look like some-one you've once loved or stopped loving. I don't think anybody fully understands what it's like resembling someone you wish you didn't love anymore. I feel like I'm carrying a face full of omens these days. Every time I look into the mirror, I remember my slow brush with death. I remembered dadi, all plain and wrinkled. Dadi's face looked like a wake for years.

&

I tend to scratch my face until I'm bleeding. I dress up in Band-Aids the way one carries a bouquet and I feel pathetic for it. I hate how noticeable everything is in a bandage: the proof of ache. Oh, it hurts. Oh, I think I'm dying. Oh, I don't think you understand. Oh, please look at me. Oh god, don't look at me. Oh, please do not pretend to understand. Oh, I need you to dress my wounds with your eyes. Oh, I'm not sure my pain is digestible anymore. Oh, look at me once more before you turn away.

&

I'm terrified of moving in with my partner. I'm terrified of them coming home to find me dying or wanting to die. I hate how when we're close they can smell death through my clothes. This is why I'm careful to maintain distance. This is why I'm afraid of balconies. I have stood on a balcony and I've felt closer to god than I've ever felt in bed with a man. Did Loona ever feel this way? I feel ridiculous talking about sex and death in the same breath. But less ridiculous than talking about death alone.

&

I'm young and I'm supposed to want to live. I'm supposed to want this life and I do. But I feel selfish to want to scream for whatever good I've been offered and thinking it's not enough. Others have it worse, my parents always consoled themselves. I couldn't think of it like that. I couldn't think of joy, its punchline and constant refrain, without recognizing its relentless absence. It feels particularly humiliating to go on some days as if being told, *do you really think you deserve it?*

Or: *The relentless pursuit of happiness makes you pathetic, do you see it?*
Or: *Haven't you got better things to do?*
Or: *You're taking space, aren't you?*

It's funny because I can answer and say: I deserve this life and I'm not pathetic to want joy to be more than a memory or an invention. I'm at this life like a bone, I'm making something beautiful. But I never answer differently. I nod and offer my head.

&

My father was the first person to apologize to me.

If you've never been apologized to, let me be the one to say it: *I'm sorry.*

When my father held my face between his hands and offered an apology, I could only cry. Here was this man, so much bigger than me, wiser than me, or so I had hoped. Here was this man whom I loved so much and who showed that he loved me too. But he forgot to apologize for the important things, for things that really hurt. If I had pride, I felt that he had crushed it.

When I talk about my father, I inevitably cry. It feels like the most natural response. It feels a lot like reading a sad story in a children's book, except all this while it was my own story. Except the person who went missing was me. Maybe that explains my feelings of loss. Maybe that explains the price we pay for love. Maybe that explains nothing but that I'm waiting for him to look for me in the bathroom and remember that pain did not look good on me. I love that he remembers what I like to eat. I love that he asks me how I am doing when nobody else does. I love that he would make me breakfast to take to school and braid my hair. I miss my father more than I love him.

&

My language is a symptom of my father. My father was the first one who introduced me to Punjabi poetry. He was my introduction to Batalvi. How in his company I sang with my mouth closed and my ears all sound. My language is always my father's first, all beautiful and wretched. All bone and sometimes mercy.

&

Father, if this is love, I want mercy. Father, you told me that since you gave me life, you were right to take it away too. Father, do you still believe it? Father, do you still think I bring you shame? Father, would you hold my hand if I reached out to you? Father, if I told you that I wanted to die, would you tell me to kill myself again?

&

Father is just another word. Is that what you thought too when you ran away from the house as a child.

&

You were talking about my brother in your inside voice and you had said: *he really should kill himself instead of just talking about it every day*. My brother heard it and he didn't come out of his room for days. Father, I understand your feelings of inadequacy and your helplessness. I have felt it too, I have rushed in the middle of the night to pray on the bathroom floor to a god I didn't believe in. Father, I'm not innocent either. I have hardly kissed this life. Father, I know you've hardly left the house in years. But father, can you please come home now.

&

Loona was sixteen when she was forced to give up everything. Loona was sixteen when she was married off to King Salwan. Loona was sixteen and she was told this was the fate of a woman. Loona was sixteen and she did not think life was this cruel. Loona was sixteen and she was responsible for everything she had to give up. Loona was sixteen when Pooran died and she had loved him. Loona was sixteen and she wasn't innocent. Loona was sixteen and she had her whole life in front of her except she couldn't touch it and her hands were tied to herself. Loona was sixteen and Pooran wasn't the only one who had died.

&

Father, do you know how old I was when I had first wanted to die? I was hardly ten and my hands were the only evidence.

&

Father, if you touched and held my hand for the first time again, I don't imagine I would know the word for love. You touch me and I touch you, crying.

&

Both you and I, we need proof that our existence matters, to each other, if not the world. I know so many times you've said that you'd die eventually and that I'll miss you but I already do. Imagine me alive and happy. Imagine yourself as part of my life still. Haven't we both wanted that more than to blame history. Imagine our bodies as two poles, connecting to each other with a single line. I can hear your heartbeat, the momentum of song, of rich misspellings. To be alive at the same time is a gift we both give to each other, I to you and you to me. I want to keep giving you this gift, if you will let me.

Notes

Loona is the titular character of the story Loona, a retelling of the Pooran Bhagat qissa by Shiv Kumar Batalvi. The 'original' qissa by Kadaryar demonized Loona by portraying her as an immoral, promiscuous woman. Batalvi narrates the story through Loona's perspective in the light of her being a sixteen-year-old girl who only wished to live her life but was instead forced to marry a man much older than her.

jade vine (it/its) is a queer, transgender/agender anarchist, gender vandalist, poet, essayist, and teaching artist from Chandigarh, India. It is the author of three poetry chapbooks, namely *Heaven is Only a Part of Our Body Where All the Sickness Resides* (Ghost City Press, 2018), *The End Is Not Apocalypse But Another Morning Where Everyone Tells Me I'm Dead* (Yavanika Press, 2021), and *Everybody's Favourite Hoe & Then Some* (Ginger Bug Press, 2023). Its work has appeared in *Glass: A Journal of Poetry*, *Rust + Moth*, *Minola Review*, *Polyphony H.S*, and elsewhere. It is deeply inspired by the transformative justice movements, the politics of indispensability, and the multimedia practice of hope.

NOW AVAILABLE FROM
SPLIT/LIP PRESS

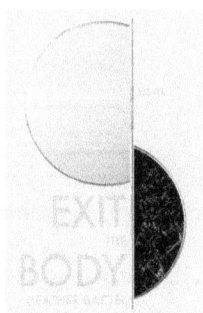

For more info about the press and titles,
visit us at www.splitlippress.com

Follow us on Instagram and Twitter: @splitlippress